D1152501

Who Am I?

Experiences of Donor Conception

With Foreword and Afterword
by
Dr Alexina McWhinnie

Idreos Education Trust

Published by Idreos Education Trust 2006
15 Wathen Road, Leamington Spa
Warwickshire CV32 5UX

idreostrust@hotmail.co.uk

ISBN 10: 0-9554031-0-3
ISBN 13: 978-0-9554031-0-1

Contents

Foreword

The contemporary debates about human reproductive technology and assisted conception provisions are about extending freedom of choice for would-be parents and avoidance of discrimination. A recent addition to this is an argument to justify less regulation of reproductive technology on the grounds of its now established successes. But is such confidence in its success justified? Does it lead to a good outcome for the families that result and particularly for the children? In fact the current emphasis is not on the outcome but on the plight of infertile adults. Conspicuous by their absence in the debate are the children created by these new techniques.

What follows is an exploration of how these children fare, in particular those conceived from donor insemination. What are the consequences for them in the short and long term? Are there psychological, emotional and ethical issues for them resulting from their being created through a clinical procedure: insemination of a fertile woman with the sperm of an unknown man, a stranger to her, to her partner and of course to the child?

Many argue that to be wanted and loved will be enough to make a happy child result. Is such an argument valid? Only those who have experienced donor conception first-hand really know. That is why this publication is of such crucial importance.

The life histories that follow all come from the first generation of donor-conceived people, now in their 30s, 40s and 50s. Reading these histories will give you an inside picture of these people's experiences and thoughts. These issues should be part of any contemporary debate about possible changes in the law, including the downgrading of the Welfare of the Child clause[1] in the current act together with a

---

[1] The Human Fertilisation and Embryology Act 1990, chapter 37, Section 13 (5): "A woman shall not be provided with treatment services unless account has been taken of the welfare of any child who may be born as a result of the treatment (including the need of that child for a father), and of any other child who may be affected by the birth." The Act and provisions came into operation on 1 August 1991.

general reduction in the degree of regulation of medical practice in this area. The contributors are as much stakeholders or more so than those currently being consulted.

If you were to meet any of the contributors you would find them competent, caring, thoughtful women, carrying on their normal lives like anyone else in the community, with their own personalities and style of humour. What you would not know on meeting them in everyday life is the inner world that they have to deal with every day and the emotional problems and turmoil that being a donor-conceived person has brought to them. Their stories, told in their own individual way, will give you a picture of this. And they are not unique in their stories nor in the issues they raise. These are mirrored in the life histories and experiences of the increasing number of donor-conceived adults now willing and able to write or speak publicly about their experience and to discuss these issues on the internet and with the media. They are thus available to be consulted.

What is relevant and important is that the themes raised illustrate vividly the same themes that appear in each generation of donor-conceived adults. These have not changed no matter what the changes in medical practice have been.

The other actors in these families are, of course, the parents. In the Afterword, what is available and known about their attitudes and their relationships will be described.

Kinship: are some more equal than others?

Joanna Rose

I was conceived by donor insemination thirty-two years ago. My social father was a doctor and my mother a nurse. I was raised with my brother (I think, genetically my half-brother through donor insemination) in London. We led a fairly eventful life. My family were pretty unconventional, not just in regard to the use of donor insemination, but less controversially in their wonderful sense of humour and adventure.

We were not very different from many other donor families. There was little acknowledgment of the fact that our family was created from, and included, an anonymous man/men, nor of the fact that we knew of no other families that were donor-conceived.

So we lived our lives as if we were the same as everyone else – as if we were all genetically related. "What donor"? we would have said if we could, but we didn't because we acted as though he did not exist. We were sensitive to the issues that lay beneath the surface, affecting all of our identities; for example, the fragility my brother and I perceived in relation to our Dad's infertility. This was coupled with my mother's belligerent wish to continue in "her" family as though everything was "fine" and as if the undercurrents of complexity weren't there. My mother had achieved genetic parenthood; she was as satisfied as she could be (with an infertile husband), but it was quite different for my Dad. In essence, he was our adoptive father, and this for him created very different and isolating parenting experiences.

Undercurrents

My brother's and my own traits became politicised by these sensitivities. I felt confusion at my appearance and wanted to look less like I did, and be more like the family that surrounded me. My brother perceived himself to have a different racial origin, but we tried to deal with these things quietly, by ourselves. The uncomfortable aspects of our lives were tiptoed around.

All families have undercurrents, but ours were beyond the average experience, and mostly beyond communication. The vessel of our family had a crack that threatened to sink us, so we tried to sail and tread very carefully. None of our friends lived with these issues; there was an otherness about us and our lives.

Finally, my parents divorced – the boat split, and we went in different directions. While wanting to share the complexity of my experience, I will not expose all the sadness and dysfunction that occurred; suffice it to say that boarding school was a safe, but regrettable outcome. Still we struggled with issues that remained unresolved. This contradicts the common assumption that the mere desire to have children necessarily equates to good family support for children of reproductive technology. At 19 I went to Australia, still unaware of why I was so uncomfortable with myself, but determined to gain the space and time I needed to understand myself better. I was suffering from bulimia and repeated bouts of depression: confused about my identity, and unable to decide what I liked or who I was. I had internalised the discomfort and did not know why I felt so bad.

Genetic bewilderment

Now, after years of reflection and interaction with other donor-conceived adults and with adoptees, I have gained the understanding I was searching for. I was suffering from what is known as "genetic bewilderment". The simplicity that we were trying to live by, as though we were the same as everyone else, was finally laid to rest, and I started to face the complexity of my life. I realised that my features were not just "different" and disappointingly unlike the ones around me, but were probably shared with people I did not know. I then allowed myself to think about my genetic father and to want to know who he was – what his face was like, if that was where I got mine from. I felt grief and loss at not being related to the Dad who raised me and for not having his interesting, familiar and culturally rich heritage. I was no longer Jewish in ancestry; I grieved that not only was I not Jewish, but had nothing to replace this heritage with, so could feel no pride in what was a blank.

I found myself with unanswered questions: I wanted to know what it would be like to look my father in the eyes. What colour eyes did he have? Were they gentle? Would I like him or he like me? I felt incensed at not knowing who my siblings were. I yearned to know about them, wondered what we had in common. I wanted to talk to them. I wondered if they were funny, or tall, or nice? I had finally allowed myself to think outside the box that had silently placed its walls around my mind. I felt a natural passion grow inside me: a passion to know about where I was from and who I was.

This need to know and acknowledge who I was hurt my parents: they had bouts of anger and confusion in reaction to it. I felt glad to have the geographical distance between us, to help protect and buffer us all from the intensity of the emotions being raised. I could not help it, but my newly acquired psychological freedom threatened both my parents: my father in his infertility and my mother in her "simplicity". I felt that my mother's side of the family were primarily concerned for her: loyalties were pitted against each other. I also faced the fact that my brother had been trying to find his own roots for ten years before me, and that I had tried to protect my Dad from what I perceived as my brother's insensitive rejection of us. Sadly, I had not understood why my brother had needed to do this. My lack of understanding and support for him at that time had caused distance and anger between us.

Politics

I still go to conferences and hear others refer to the use of donor gametes as a "medical treatment" or "infertility intervention", with the idea they will be "building" a "normal" family that then "gets on with life". The speaker frequently asserts that families come in different shapes and sizes – all of which must (apparently) be intentionally created and accepted. The simplicity and convenience of this gloss, created and projected from heartfelt aspirations, is familiar to me.

Now the trend is changing slightly: support groups run by awakening parents of donor offspring, research and advocacy, along with a High Court case, have led to more recognition of donor conception as having something in common with adoption, opening the door to some acknowledgement of kinship loss and identity confusion. There is at least some more discussion of the topic.

Clearly, donor conception is contentious and political. People are very passionate about it and refer in debate to "reproductive rights", and to the dwindling supply of gametes. It is nature versus nurture, those for and against, with the emotional vitriol found elsewhere in the context of euthanasia and abortion. I have contributed to the debate. I was involved in the High Court case on donor anonymity and am in the process of writing a PhD addressing the ethics (or absence thereof), kinship and identity issues raised by donor conception. There are legal and academic arguments that go to the core of what it is to be human; to be a parent; what constitutes a family; where liberty ends and harm begins. I feel compelled to follow and engage in the debate. But more than anything, I *feel* the debate, whether I want to or not; I *live* in that complex and contentious arena.

Secrecy

Some think that if the nature of our conception is denied, we are spared this complexity. But I know of too many people who suffered from secrecy and lies in their families. I know of too many who were relieved to finally find out the truth – their truth – not least in relation to false medical histories, unexplained traits, features, sensitivities and atmospheres. I now live with the absence of knowledge relating to half my medical history, ethnicity and genetic kin. This is preferable to and less dangerous than false knowledge, but by no means something that should have been deliberately constructed by medical professionals bound by the Hippocratic principle of "do no harm".

Reproductive technology has embarked on an experiment on me and others. I am one of the guinea-pigs, telling you the results of this experiment on me. Such "results" are hardly sought by the fertility industry. However, in spite of this, there has been mounting pressure for change, and some mistakes have been conceded. In the future, information about the donor and associated kinship will be available to those who are told of their donor conception, but this all depends on others: the power and judgment are out of the offspring's hands. Many will not be told, and their rights and identities are not protected from this deceit about their kinship and origins.

4

In fact, in the UK, most offspring will not be told of the nature of their conception (currently at least 85% are not told) and will be raised among the undercurrents with no name or explanation – just left to guess. I hold those who condone and facilitate this practice complicit in harmful deception of people like myself. They are complicit in a practice that has led to our deliberately created kinship confusion, and to misleading information being on our birth certificates, along with misinformation regarding our medical histories.

Tracing relatives

As for me, in the last ten years I have found three very likely contenders to be my genetic relatives. There have been many other possibilities too. I frequently receive messages from donor offspring, who send their photos and ask if I look like them. Who knows who I am related to? I certainly don't. I have had two self-funded genetic tests to try to get some answers.

One of my potential fathers from the clinic at 52 Harley Street, Dr Beeney, tells me that the students he knows of, those involved at the time and place of my conception, had tried to "corner the market". His honesty and information are refreshing – but yet he tells me that this handful referred to the clinics as the "wank bank". The young students had "cornered the markets" of three clinics in the vicinity, and as a now respected and qualified doctor, he estimates that he, and each of his friends, have between one and three *hundred* children. Beeney (1999) has since written a book and has re-evaluated his actions. He has clearly been deeply troubled by the biological and moral consequences of his naïve choices. He made the mistake of treating his reproductive material as on a par with blood to be donated – the more the merrier.

For me, the emotional and ethical issues that have been raised by trying to track down my genetic family, now thought to be, with half siblings, in the hundreds, carries enormous, and arguably equally consuming effects as having to face infertility itself. But I notice that the pain and emotional anguish of infertility takes front stage. The complex and difficult realities created to alleviate this pain recede into the background. Government funding for the National Gamete Donation Trust advances the notion that gamete donation is akin to

5

blood donation, undermining my, and Dr Beeney's, lived experience in one brief, uninformed stroke.

Double standards

The contradictions inherent in an industry that seeks to provide the maximum in genetic continuity for its customers, yet routinely treats the genetic kinship of the offspring and donors as expendable, are blinding. There is outrage at IVF blunders, and we see fertility interventions for people with AIDS[1] and intracytoplasmic sperm injection (ICSI) to facilitate conception with immotile sperm, along with various interventions to help cancer sufferers to achieve "the unlimited aim of enabling an individual to become a parent of a genetically related child".[2] In case there is any doubt about precisely why these interventions are provided, ICSI "may help [patients] father their own genetically healthy children". Apparently "All these new developments may leave little room for AID (artificial insemination by donor) as a means of alleviating infertility in many couples".[3] Implicit in the reasoning as to why AID may one day be superseded is that it is primarily a last resort for those who have given up on their first preference: that of having their own genetic children. This is supported by the following research: "Among the 128 couples in whom the male partner was oligozoospermic... 36 never underwent ICSI because they had an AID child before ICSI was available... Ninety-two patients opted for AID after an ICSI attempt, mainly because the procedure had failed".[4]

I am left to conclude that double standards exist. There are those "produced" who are told they should be grateful to be alive, with the suggestion that they should have minimal regard for their own genetic continuity – a malleable regard, to be controlled and directed by others. Yet those who approach the industry are supported to maximise their own genetic continuity with future offspring, even when this creates a corresponding loss for the offspring. Unlike the offspring, these

---

[1] Charles and Spriggs, 2003.
[2] British Fertility Society, 2002, p. 5.
[3] Vernaeve, Festre *et al*, 2005, p. 26.
[4] Ibid, p. 22.

people are apparently not expected to be appeased by the fact they are alive and should be "grateful" for that. There are similarities with the justifications made in support of battery farming: those who have known of no other conditions than the ones they have been created for should not expect or want greater fulfilment or equality. They would not be alive were it not for this practice, which supposedly justifies and necessitates its acceptance.

As a further instance of double standards, those who support the significance of the donor-conceived offspring's genetic kinship are invariably asked to provide the impossible: statistical data from a secretly-produced population. They are challenged to prove that more offspring are harmed by this enforced kinship absence than are not. Such requirements are never made of those who seek their kinship continuity through reproductive technology. The value of this continuity is treated as a given, as it is for the rest of society.

Multiple parents

My mother has now remarried – not unusual for many, but now I have four fathers: a genetic (donor) father, a social father, and now a step-father; then there is my brother's father too. With divorce rates as they are, I wonder how many "parents" children from the IVF industry will have to cope with. The familial complexity continues to expand outwards with the intergenerational aftermath from short-sighted and ill-considered attempts to resolve one problem: infertility. For many, counselling is advanced as a virtual elixir for IVF-created families. Yet the question of whose genetic relationships matter, and how much, is not an easy one to "negotiate". The meaning of innate has been pulled from under our feet, and we are left to the uncertainty of individual interpretations and high emotions.

And so it continues: social, gestational and genetic parenthood are fractured, rearranged and given changing levels of significance. The fertility industry has introduced a kinship of commissioning intention, which is presented to the public as though it were a simple solution. But the unity found in the "glue" that holds people together, and creates a sense of intergenerational connection and responsibility, is being exploited and left to the control of one or two people, on the basis of what is present or absent in their own reproductive capacity. All other family members, those inside and outside of the acknowledged circle (both donor relatives and non-genetic relatives), are expected to accept and live within the confines of the commissioners' intentions throughout their lifetimes. This is an unrealistic expectation.

Genetic ties

All these families live in a broader society, in which there is significance in looking like one's relatives. Indeed, familial resemblance is one of the first things people look for and comment on when seeing a newborn. I notice that many people love to talk about their ancestry. Further, genetics is contributing more and more to our knowledge of medicine. The paradox is simple and clear to me. Yet society is encouraged to turn a blind eye to the inherent discrimination involved in kinship construction and destruction via use of donor gametes. It is a type of empathetic blindness, encouraged and appealed for by the infertile, the fertility industry and its advocates. It is fuelled not just by the personal convictions of those in the industry, but by that industry's undeniable profits. The donor offspring are made to order, to fit a design; they are the next best thing to having one's own genetic child, and they are presented and objectified as something to which someone else has a right.

It is commonly argued that other donor offspring would say they were delighted by the intervention that allowed them to exist, and their parents to have a family. There are some donor offspring who would have few complaints. In reply, I would assert that I also know of infertile people who accepted their infertility, and are also happy with their current lives. Infertility is not something that *has* to be appeased at all costs, and these arguments do not address the inherent ethical problems.

Instead of playing battleships with statistics painfully established after the event, there are important social values and principles which should be respected. Individuals, institutions and governments need to ask whether they wish to treat kinship as flexible and open to interpretation, but only for particular members of society, when and how it suits them. Do they wish to be complicit in creating a special class or underclass of people whose kinship is given less protection or regard than that of other members? Is the erosion of role, connection,

8

and responsibility between blood relatives something to encourage? Will this have a broader corrosive effect?

Best interests of child

There is a benefit to be found in looking at practices where genetic continuity has been fractured with some greater good in mind. Indeed, this is not the first time this has happened. The lessons from adoption, and here in Australia of the "stolen generations" (involving the deliberate break-up of Aboriginal families), have overwhelmingly contradicted the notion that genetic kinship is something that should be fractured for any other reason than as a last resort *for the child*. This is hard-earned wisdom. Removing a child from its genetic family is an intervention now performed only to protect the child's best interests. No more is it accepted to address other problems, or promote other ideals. Institutions should never promote and facilitate such fracturing as a means to other people's ends.

Just as infertility is grieved, because people grieve the loss of having and raising their own genetic children, so too can that loss be mirrored by not knowing or being raised by one's own genetic parents. Indeed, for many, this loss is exacerbated when it is intentionally and institutionally created, unlike infertility. Such kinship loss is recognised as having a negative statistical impact on the health and well-being of adoptees, who are over-represented in most forms of crisis care.[5] Further, this loss has been identified by leaders in the field as having a lifelong impact.[6] This has also been found to be the case in relation to problems created for members of the stolen generations.[7]

To support an industry that ignores this evidence, and demotes the best interests of the child from "paramount" to "taken into account" seems recklessly indifferent to the vulnerability and equality of those so produced. If some people still hold genuine doubts as to whether genetic kinship is less important than is currently believed, then I oppose actively experimenting on the kinship of those who are

---

[5] Lifton, 1994.
[6] Triseliotis, 1973.
[7] ATSIC, 2002.

unable to negotiate on their own behalf. Clearly, those who approach the services of the fertility industry do not agree with this perceived unimportance, as "90% of couples choose to discard their spare embryos. Surveys show that one reason that so few embryos are donated is that couples attach great significance to genetic parenthood".[8] Why assume that those commissioned into existence would not also "attach great significance to genetic parenthood", particularly if they were raised with these values embedded in the psyche of their parents and society at large?

I know personally what it is like to be experimented on, and those involved got it wrong: I have experienced considerable hurt as a consequence. Those responsible did not safeguard what I have become increasingly aware of as important to me.

To intentionally create life carries with it grave responsibility. Admittedly, there are many who are naturally conceived and who are also deceived and denied knowledge of their genetic kinship. However, to use the worst-case scenario on the street as a benchmark for setting standards of professional practice, which are then seen as "good enough", is ethically bankrupt. We would not accept standards such as these with other forms of medical intervention, allowing professionals and institutions to provide care similar to that provided by untrained and uninformed members of the general public. Yet reproductive technology utilises these types of justification that would be unacceptable in any other context. Certainly, they would be rejected in the case of adoption, or other social institutions responsible for the care of children, where children's kinship and best interests are paramount, not just "taken into account".

Despite the sense of injustice I feel, I want to say that I am deeply committed and connected to my family. We are bound together by a love that is crucial, and yet thankfully it is not now a love that renders me speechless on issues that affect me so directly. Such stifling loyalty, leaving people incapable of critically analysing their situation, is something I would not wish on my worst enemy. It is not the stuff of genuine relationships.

---

[8] Fuscaldo and Savulescu, 2005.

Experiences of absence

In the face of my predicament, I find it cathartic to illustrate the irony created by the selective acknowledgement of genetic ties and to explain the stinging pain that this creates. I know that through doing so I am also providing some warning of the pain that is being created on a daily basis by the fertility industry. Amongst the donor offspring I know who recognise this inequality, we refer to such experiences as "salt stories". These are stories where what was intentionally rendered absent to us is obliviously enjoyed in our presence: for many this rubs salt in our wounds. As you can imagine, the world can be one big salt pit for those deeply sensitised by these haunting absences.

Simply seeing other people, including family members, with their fathers, experiencing continuity with their kinfolk, continuity with their paternal connection; hearing people talk of their ancestral history and lineage, makes me think of my own genetic grandparents and relatives, and wonder if I look or act like any of them. I cannot tell which bits of me are mine alone and which come from my lost heritage. I wonder if any of my paternal relatives know of or imagine my existence. How many know of my genetic father's intergenerationally-affecting activities? I think of the judgment from my court case[9] that finally ascertained in law that we donor offspring have the same rights to information concerning our identities as anyone else. Yet I know from experience that these rights are not recognised, due to the very nature of donor conception.

Psychological harms

Donor conception has been introduced first by stealth, in the face of public opposition, as a secret practice, and then it uncloaked itself and demanded acceptance on the basis that it existed and is expected by some. The serious public debate about whether this is something that should be promoted, funded and facilitated by government institutions has been leapfrogged. Also needing re-evaluation is the perception and management of donor conception as a medical rather than a social

---

[9] Rose and Another v. Secretary of State for Health and Human Fertilisation and Embryology Authority (2002) WHC 1593.

intervention. The assessment of harms is skewed by this medical mindset. Suicide is a major killer in Western society, despite the physical health of many tragically lost in this way. It is vital for psychosocial health to be considered no less important than physical health in assessment of, and accountability for, the harms created by donor conception.

Increasing numbers of donor offspring experience the aftermath of living in secretive families, and/or having fractured kinship and genetic bewilderment. The erosion of respect for people's kinship and equality in relation to a select group in society has regressive parallels with slavery. Whether the various defences of this "exclusive", "special" and inequitable treatment for donor offspring are driven by pragmatic reasons or just blind empathy for the infertile, the result is one that I appeal to you to confront. There are many ways to be created and conceived; not all should be supported, let alone facilitated and promoted.

Creating life and parenthood are understandable ends to aspire to, but the means of doing so must remain under scrutiny. To place the pain of infertility, rather than the interests of the child, as paramount is a retrograde social step. To seek to excuse this by asserting that those so produced should be grateful to be "wanted" and "loved", or even to exist, is a dangerous way to think and will lead to inevitable and increasing assaults on the identities of future generations. The burden of infertility must not be circumvented by ill-considered quick fixes that pass the baton of grief and loss to the next generation. One can paralyse the expression of this loss – disenfranchise it – but that will not take it away. The consequences are serious and deserve more consideration.

If infertility is to be considered, and responded to, as an objective and lamentable loss, then for reasons of equity and consistency, the mirror image of this loss for the next generation should not then be presented as something to be willingly created and responded to with indifference. Those who do so are either blind to their own hypocrisy, or happy to endorse the creation of a type of underclass to serve the utility and desires of others.

REFERENCES

Aboriginal and Torres Strait Islander Commission (ATSIC), About link-up services. Retrieved 6 November 2002 from http://www.atsic.

gov.au/issues/law_and_justice/bringing_them_home_report/task_force/about_linkup.asp

Beeney, M (1999) *Children of Eden*, The Book Guild, Lewes

British Fertility Society (2002) A strategy for fertility services for survivors of childhood cancer. Retrieved 7 January 2005 from http://www.britishfertilitysociety.org.uk/practicepolicy/documents/fccpaper.pdf

Charles, T, Spriggs, M (2003) HIV and assisted reproductive technologies: Should HIV discordant couples have access to assisted reproductive technologies? *Journal of Medical Ethics* **29**, pp. 325–329

Fuscaldo, G, Savulescu, J (2005) Spare embryos: 3000 reasons to rethink the significance of genetic relatedness. *Reproductive BioMedicine Online* **10**, pp. 164–168

IVF blunder alert system, BBC News UK edition, 5 June 2003. Retrieved 25 November 2004 from http://news.bbc.co.uk/1/hi/health/2965508.stm

Lifton, Betty-Jean (1994) *Journey of the adopted self: A quest for wholeness,* Basic Books, New York

Rose and Another v. Secretary of State for Health and Human Fertilisation and Embryology Authority (2002) WHC 1593

Triseliotis, J P (1973) *In search of origins: The experiences of adopted people*, Routledge & Kegan Paul, London

Vernaeve, V, Festre, V *et al* (2005) Reproductive decisions by couples undergoing artificial insemination with donor sperm for severe male infertility: implications for medical counselling. *International Journal of Andrology* **28**, pp. 22–26

Worrying the wound: the hidden scars of donor conception

Christine Whipp

Revisiting a less-than-idyllic childhood might be seen as the intellectual equivalent of picking an old scab and watching it bleed, but such a journey, when accomplished with hindsight, can sometimes be the best way to make sense of the past, lay ghosts to rest and proceed with optimism into the future. I have, since happening on the strange truth about my personal circumstances, been prepared to openly share elements of my own upbringing and life experiences in the hope of enabling others to understand the injustices and problems that can arise from unnatural beginnings.

The beauty of hindsight is that it allows us to see the past with an enlightened perspective, but while I was frantically busy living my life, I was not aware that it was noticeably different from or more disadvantaged than those of my contemporaries. There was no way of comparing the timbre of their lives with my own. Married in the bleak days of post-war Britain, my mother worked in the local net factory and my father was a carpenter in the family business. They were well-known members of the community in a small rural market town. Seven years into their union my anticipated arrival was set to be the icing on their marital cake, but my life got off to an inauspicious start. Hugely pregnant and unwilling to wait any longer, my mother walked to the steep summit of Bottom Woods, then deliberately jump-started my delivery by running down again. Just after midnight on 1 April 1955 I was thrust into the world, looking like a skinned rabbit. I was more of an April Fool than people would have guessed. My father, who was a hard-working, unassuming man with a dry wit, registered my birth. My name, nationality and place in society were secured.[1]

Separateness

It is hard to say, or be in any way precise about, the age at which I began to feel that something unseen and unspoken was pervading my life, just as it is simply impossible to describe the tense aura of "something-is-going-to-happen" or to articulate the feeling of separateness I endured as a child: one which to some extent I still do to this day. I think these sensations were always there and I was always aware of them, if at first only subconsciously. I was about three years old when my diabetic father suddenly went blind. We spent time together while he listened to the radio and his "talking books" and I played quietly or tended to any requests involving simple tasks. His health deteriorated as renal failure took its toll, but he bore his illness and disability with uncomplaining dignity. He spent time away, firstly in hospital, then later at a rehabilitation centre. After a period as a wheelchair-bound invalid, he died in hospital when I was just six years old.

My mother did not encourage me to mourn for my father. The funeral took place without my knowledge, and I grieved for the man I called Daddy in private. I should have provided a comfort to my widowed mother, who juggled part-time jobs, battled with bills and coped with life's general problems, but as a child in a one-parent family, I had a complex and difficult relationship with my mother during my formative years. Beneath her capable exterior she was a cauldron of frustration, anger and resentment. She had expectations of me which I was rarely able to meet, and on the few occasions when I excelled at anything she would bask in the reflected glory in public but seethe with jealousy behind closed doors. She was both critical and controlling. No matter how hard I tried, I was never able to please her. I soon learnt that my best option was always to appease her and go along with whatever she wanted rather than visibly attempt to plough my own furrow.

---

[1] The small print at the foot of a birth certificate reads: "It is an offence to falsify a certificate or to make or knowingly use a false certificate or copy of a false certificate intending it to be accepted as genuine to the prejudice of any person, or to possess a certificate knowing it to be false without lawful authority."

In quiet moments I would sometimes ponder on the unfathomable atmosphere of "impending happentude" which I found so deeply unsettling. I could only identify that there was something around me that was not quite right. It, My Mother, Me, Life, all of these things and none of them were clouded and tainted, but by what, I could not exactly define. Somewhere along the way I had developed the idea that everything sad and bad that had happened in my life was my fault: retribution for a past misdeed which I was not aware of having committed, a deed which had invoked my mother's long-term wrath and displeasure. I had become deeply religious for a while, in the hope that being more spiritual and saintly might reverse what seemed to be a tragic trend. It felt as if my life was misplaced and that I was out of kilter with my surroundings. I even dallied with the idea that I wasn't "the right me" when the notion hit me during a primary school geography lesson that the stork who brought me must have got confused at the equator and dropped me in darkest Dorset instead of directly down under in New Zealand. There was something so disconcerting in that thought that I filed it away and refused to revisit it until I was much older, but not, as it happens, that much wiser.

My mother's second marriage in 1964 brought me a step-father, a new surname, a host of different and thankfully welcoming "family" members, and even a new baby half-sister. Outsiders might think I ought to have been jealous that the tiny newcomer had imposed upon my exclusive relationship with my mother, but I felt nothing but gratitude for all the attention she lavished on the baby. I was suddenly less under permanent critical scrutiny. I settled down to my studies at the local comprehensive and gradually developed a surprisingly good relationship with my step-father, whose respectful friendship and quiet encouragement was a stabilizing influence in my teenage years. My mother continued to be disdainful and hyper-critical, particularly of my boyfriend, of whom she strongly disapproved. Then I went unforgivably off the rails and got pregnant just before taking my "A" levels. I was married to my soul-mate and living with him and our baby daughter on a shoe-string budget before my 19th birthday.

Partial revelation

My mother was less able to dominate my life when my husband and I and our two children moved away from my home town, but she continued to manipulate everyone and everything around her and was happy to paint me in a poor light whenever possible. Everything I did continued to displease her. We visited her on an almost weekly basis, and at one such gathering when the family were seated at Sunday tea, talking loudly amongst themselves, she shot an angry glance at me before hissing accusingly the now immortal words: *There is something about your past which you don't know.* For one precious moment a pinpoint of light flashed in the dark of my inner confusion, but full enlightenment was not then to be. My mother refused to expand further on the subject. Instinctively I knew that this partial revelation pointed to the source of all her animosity towards me and also that I would have to wait patiently until *she* deemed it a satisfactory time for all to be revealed.

My relationship with my mother plummeted to new depths after my step-father died. Her thinly-veiled antagonism towards me had become open hostility, and I was no longer made to feel welcome at the bungalow where I had grown up, and where my half-sister and her fiancé lived. Encouraged by my husband, I ventured to question my mother on why she was persistently behaving so scornfully towards me, even deliberately lying to me when it suited her. In a fit of explosive rage she once again threw the tantalising secret of my past at me and claimed she would reveal everything in a letter after she died. This point was a watershed in our relationship and it became obvious that there was no future in that relationship unless I was prepared to continue accepting the level of psychological abuse and lack of respect which she had meted out over the years. I broke free, knowing that there was most definitely a secret. I was that secret, but my mother and the grudge she bore was part of the secret too.

Guesswork

One possible explanation that I had long been exploring, having pieced together fragments of information with the aid of intuition, was that my paternity might be in question. There was my late father's dark hair and eye colouring which defied the accepted laws of biological inheritance; the case of teenage mumps that spelled potential infertility; the diabetes which causes impotence and the underlying impression that, as solid and respectable as my paternal ancestors had been, I was just not one of them. My mother had always remarked on the strong physical similarities between the two of us, but I could not see them myself and increasingly felt, as I grew older and less sharp-faced with age, that I didn't particularly resemble anyone in my supposed family either in looks or disposition. I thought back to the mis-directional stork and pondered. I knew that I had not been adopted, because I had met the kindly old town midwife who delivered me, and my full birth certificate stated that I was the child of my mother and her husband. Much as this piece of paper is supposed to be a foolproof legal document, I refused to accept the words written on it, and suspected an official conspiracy. I accepted that my gut-feeling might be interpreted by others as paranoia, but I knew my mother would not have had an affair, and eventually settled on the plausible hypothesis that she had been raped, but decided to keep me, as this would fittingly account for a local cover-up, her distaste for all matters sexual and her acute dislike of me.

Revelation

I worried that as one last act of spite my mother would fail to leave the letter promised on her death. When she reached 70 I sent her a birthday card with a letter promising never to bother her again if she would just tell me the truth about the secret. It was a compromise which she was willing to accept. In a cold, stark letter she bade me appreciate that it had been very difficult for her to write. She told me that she had gone to Exeter for "Artificial Insemination by Donor". It had taken "a long time and a lot of distress and heartache". Although I knew very little about infertility treatment, apart from the arrival in 1978 of Louise Brown, the first "test-tube baby", I was ready to accept this unexpected revelation as the truth. My mother could never have invented such a bizarre story. For me this letter provided a "Eureka" moment in which everything suddenly made sense. At the age of 41, I was effectively reborn. There I was, on an otherwise ordinary November morning, walking through middle age with a face I had never met. My ancestral home was a glass sample jar, and my parents never knew one another in either the personal or the biblical sense. I couldn't name a single person who shared this strange science-fiction style background, and found myself feeling more alone and completely separate from the rest of the human race than I had ever felt before.

The bare facts alone were hideously opposed to anything I had ever believed in. An anonymous sperm donor had provided a woman gynaecologist with a sample of his most intimate bodily fluids, in the full knowledge that his masturbatory activities could result in the birth of a child, his child, who would be brought up by strangers. My existence owed almost nothing to the serendipitous nature of normal human reproduction, where babies are the natural progression of mutually fulfilling adult relationships, but rather it represented a verbal contract, a financial transaction and a cold, clinical harnessing of medical technology. No wonder my traits and interests did not mesh with those of my mother, for while her blood group may have been compatible with that of the donor, I suspect that their personalities and values would have been very different. In real life my parents would probably never had moved in the same circles, let alone had anything resembling a relationship, so in turn, some of my inherited characteristics are a conflicting, unruly mish-mash. I am a hymn-singing atheist and shy extrovert, who can speak confidently with anyone yet sits in the corner at parties. With so much of my personality diametrically opposed to itself, and having been deprived of the influence of those who exhibited the opposing traits, there was little doubt in my mind that I grew to be only half the person I might have been.

On reading the letter, I was swept up in a maelstrom of emotions, of which elation and triumph were initially high on the list. It was actually satisfying to discover that I had been absolutely right to question my identity and suspect subterfuge. I had not been bordering on schizophrenia. I really was somebody else: the person named on my birth certificate but not the person described on it. Half of my ancestry had been signed away, and the loss of my true identity was the price I paid for my parents' reproductive compromise. It was a relief to find that nothing I had done had been to blame for my mother's irrational behaviour towards me. I was not a bad person. So many otherwise perplexing things seemed to fall into place. I felt astonishment at the level of secrecy involved in the fait-accompli, followed by a deepening sense of anger and injustice when I gradually began to realise the full implications. I had been cheated out of a relationship with my real father and paternal relatives during my formative years, and unlike

19

adoptees, who in the 1970s had been given the legal right to access their full birth information on reaching maturity, I was denied the right to have any knowledge of my father's identity, ancestry or medical history even if records existed.[2] As outrageous as it might seem, until the establishment in 1991 of the Human Fertilisation and Embryology Authority, neither the medical profession nor successive governments had seen fit to centrally catalogue the conceptions of people like me. The legacy of other people's choices did not sit easily with me as I began to address that all-important question: who am I? I vowed to make it my business to find out!

Research

Effectively, the whole of my life had been founded on a lie peddled by my parents, who commissioned my conception through the pioneering gynaecologist Dr Margaret Jackson.[3] She was not concerned that my social father-to-be was a 42-year-old insulin-dependent diabetic who stood a statistically poor chance of seeing his wife's donor-conceived baby reach adulthood. My frenzied research soon indicated that I am just one of an estimated 12,000 donor-conceived adults born in the UK prior to 1991 and one of only a small minority who have been informed of this unenviable truth about themselves. It seemed sinister to me that so many people had been so deviously and resoundingly deceived about their true selves by parents who were assured by fertility practitioners that there was no need for anyone ever to know what had happened in the consulting room. I discovered that 483 babies had been born between 1940 and 1983 as a result of donor insemination performed by Dr Margaret Jackson and that there was a distinct possibility that some of them would be my half-siblings, along with the legal children of the sperm donor himself. I looked at the faces of strangers in the supermarket queue with new interest. I wondered if I had ever unknowingly glimpsed my donor offspring peers or my biological father or any of my paternal relatives as I shopped in Exeter.

---

[2] Anyone revealing the identity of a gamete donor would, I believe, be liable, under current legislation, to a £3,000 fine or 6 months imprisonment.

[3] See Snowden, Mitchell and Snowden, 1983.

If my mother had thought her bombshell would reduce me to a wreck, she was mistaken. Anger is so often a catalyst which leads to change, and my anger had a moral dimension to it. I could not understand how the pioneers of AID[4] had thought it possible to translate the breeding principles of animal husbandry into the more complex arena of human relationships and "family building". How could they justify something which seemed so morally wrong? Why should the pain of the childlessness of one generation take precedence over the needs and rights of the next? The more I reflected on my upbringing and read about donor conception, the more it became apparent that the accepted view of this supposedly benign medical practice was at best simplistic and at worst, deliberately distorted by those with kudos, money and possibly even guilty consciences at stake. During my life-time, infertility had become big business. The introduction of IVF had enabled a circumvention of female infertility, allowing the use of donor eggs and even embryos which effectively created donor foundlings with no biological connection to the people who appeared to be their parents. Those who had been put in place to oversee the reproductive revolution were doing a woefully inadequate job. The tail was wagging the dog, and the HFEA, a quango which favored the aspirations of the infertile above the loosely-defined best interests of their intended children, had little bark and no bite. I felt compelled, as one of the few people in the position of having first-hand knowledge of the unspoken consequences of donor conception, to speak out openly and question the status quo.

Publicity

As uncharacteristic as it might have seemed of Christine the ordinary mother and housewife, Christine the "Adult Donor Offspring" ventured into the media spotlight. My aim was three-fold. Firstly, having been able to recognise from my own experiences the toxic effects of deception on my upbringing, I wanted to draw attention to the damage secrecy can cause in families resulting from this extreme

---

[4] AID (Artificial Insemination by Donor) later came to be known as DI (Donor Insemination) with the advent of HIV infection and a desire to downplay any public perception of artificiality. It is now sometimes called DC (Donor Conception), which embraces the use of donated sperm, eggs or embryos.

remedy for infertility. If donor conception was going to continue as a medically endorsed practice I felt it was imperative for openness to prevail. Secondly, I needed to draw attention to the unjustifiable identity discrimination and negative effects of donor anonymity faced by the people who resulted from it. Thirdly, I tentatively hoped that my father would generously come forward and fill in the gaps in my self-knowledge. The experience has undoubtedly been cathartic, but I have to admit that initially I was surprised at the level of hostility directed at me by some members of the pro-donor gamete lobby, who were not at all keen for my voice to be heard. Being publicly candid is an invitation to derision, along with calls for me and other donor offspring to be "grateful" we were born at all.

It is incredibly galling to be asked to justify wanting to know about the man who provided me with half of my DNA, when access to such information is so natural that it is simply taken for granted by everyone else. Respect for family and kinship is a fundamental part of our culture, and all of us need the stability that comes from being an integral part of a continuum. The importance of genetic relatedness cannot be downplayed. Genealogy and family history research is one of the fastest-growing pastimes, as is indicated by the popularity of the government-funded 1901 UK Census website, which initially crashed through pressure of use when it was first opened. Those who found my message particularly difficult to entertain were recipient parents of donor children (even those few who espoused openness and had opted to be honest about their children's mode of conception), who were unwilling to hear me speak of my anonymous donor as my "biological father", or even my "real father". They preferred to view the donor's role in their own family as that of a shadowy figure who had been a means to an end. They found it hard to accept that for me, and potentially for their own offspring, the donor has a more tangible meaning as a flesh-and-blood person with a personality, a life-style, a family history and an undeniable connection through his webbed toes, acne or any other identifiably inherited feature.

Shared concerns

Fortunately, while I did not find my father, my openness brought me into contact with other people who shared my concerns. There were

22

academics, social workers, infertility counselors, lawyers, journalists, Christians and adoptees who recognised the need for a change in how donation is regarded. Gradually I discovered other donor-conceived people, aged from 16 to 60, from countries right around the globe, whose life stories, emotions and experiences had many features which were uncannily close to those of my own. Our camaraderie was enabled by modern technology which let us exchange ideas and information at the touch of a mouse. We were able to support each other at times when our own families (with their complex and delicate dynamics) and friends had often failed miserably to understand our frustration and despondency, or when our polite approaches to clinics, or even to men who might have been our donor fathers, met with rude rebuffs.

In the privacy of a closed forum[5] we have been free to discuss how donor conception has impacted upon our lives. Some of us are "only" children while others have full or half siblings and in some cases, adopted siblings. Most of the older donor offspring discovered the truth about their conception when they were already mature adults, while many of the younger ones have known for most of their lives, or since their early teens. All are at different stages of their journey through assimilating the facts, the consequences and the fall-out, but for all of us there are always more questions than answers. While we would probably be seen by our respective peer groups as "ordinary, normal people", we admit in private to numerous problematic areas of our lives. Identity is a particular issue, and Turner and Coyle reported that participants in their survey "consistently reported mistrust within the family, negative distinctiveness, lack of genetic continuity, frustration in being thwarted in the search for their biological fathers and a need to talk to a significant other (i.e. someone who would understand). These experiences could be postulated as being indicative of a struggle to assimilate, accommodate and evaluate information about their new identities as donor offspring. Psychotherapists and counsellors need to be aware of these identity issues if they are to meet the needs of donor offspring within therapeutic practice."[6]

---

[5] People Conceived Via Artificial Insemination: http://groups.yahoo.com/group/PCVAI/
[6] Turner and Coyle, 2000, p. 2041.

23

We are essentially a small sub-section of a larger group of people, and it is impossible to say with certainty if we represent the majority. I can only speculate as to the likelihood of certain patterns of behaviour occurring in the rest of the unidentified donor gamete community, in terms of both recipient parents and offspring. My own feeling is that there may be a significant proliferation of parental mental illness, difficult maternal and social father relationships, general family dysfunction, and divorce. It is known that traditional adoptees are over-represented in psychiatric institutions and the criminal justice system, but there is no way of identifying our donor-conceived peers who are living in ignorance of the true facts, amongst the published figures for mental illness and criminal offences. It is similarly impossible to know how many of them are simply living in a state of inner confusion: failing to feel a deep and resonating connection to their apparent kinfolk.

Better parents?

I remember how dismissive three donor conception "experts" were when I stated that it was the donor insemination process which had caused the dysfunctional relationship between my mother and me, since her behaviour towards me stemmed directly from the way that she related to me as an acquisition. Although lacking any personal experience of donor conception, they maintained that my mother's behaviour was merely a reflection of her particular character, and were adamant that in general a DC mother would not have a bad relationship with a "much wanted" baby. I now know that plenty of other adult offspring have had difficult and unhappy relationships with overbearing, controlling mothers. Donor- conceived babies are a second-class option rather than the real deal. A recent survey shows that mothers of children born through IVF, even using their own gametes, spend more time with and relating to their children than do "ordinary" mothers. This is interpreted by the pro-repro-interventionists as meaning that they are "better" mothers. Other surveys have shown that DC fathers are more proactive with their children than natural fathers. Another interpretation would be that these parents are overcompensating, and risk suffocating their children with their zealous interaction. Not so much better parents, perhaps, as more interfering parents.

Denial

There are a small number of adult offspring who declare delight at their conceptional circumstances and report no regrets. Offspring who learn the truth before adulthood are, however, often subjected to limited openness, with family discussions being manipulated and confined to issues which do not unduly disturb the parental equilibrium. Some are required to keep the information about their conception within the close family circle as other relatives may not be aware of the facts. Just as children of divorced parents are often pressurized by their nurturing parent into certain behaviour patterns by Parental Alienation Syndrome (the mechanism of Stockholm Syndrome, by which people begin to align with the expressed views of their captors, in order to sustain their mental and physical survival), it is likely that a similar influence could be brought to bear on donor offspring who have not attained full autonomy. Offspring who claim no interest in their missing donor parent may be suffering the effects of (as I have termed it) "Repressed Parentage Syndrome" by which parents have effectively subjugated the desire for knowledge of the third party who contributed to "their" family. These are the offspring likely to be singled out by the donor gamete service providers as the most "well-balanced".

In the sixty-five years since Margaret Jackson first offered AID to private patients, this medical procedure for healthy women, which merely circumvents male infertility, has been protected by secrecy and has gained public acceptance by stealth. With no central government records until 1991, it has been impossible for empirical and longitudinal studies to be carried out into the long-term outcomes for all parties concerned. Even now, the "privacy" of patients and the continued general reluctance of couples to be transparent about their use of donor gametes (an estimated 90% of heterosexual commissioning couples are still hiding the truth from their children and wider society) mean that objective studies remain practically impossible. Fertility practitioners can ensure that of the few psychologists and social commentators given access to willing patients, all are strongly pro-donor gamete. With researchers using suspect methodology to obtain and interpret data to suit their own agenda, much of the academic literature published in this field may represent little more than advocacy masquerading as objective research.

Given the ability of commissioning parents to lie to their own families about their use of donor conception and even delude themselves, it is not hard to see how the most well-meaning researchers might be misled during interviews and arranged sessions to "observe" interactions between parents and uninformed small children. My own mother was sufficiently astute to pull the wool over anyone's eyes. Recipient mothers will either fall over themselves to paint a bed of roses or remain tight-lipped. Recipient fathers, where they exist, say very little. Many get air-brushed out of the picture after divorce, which seems to be quite commonplace in families built through assisted conception,[7] suggesting that a stable family structure may be particularly difficult in a family where the individuals have different levels of biological connectedness, on a par with step-families. The DCNetwork parent support group have provided their own published literature to enable small donor-conceived children to understand the process by which they were made, but this does not encourage the offspring to look beyond the mechanics of overcoming the sadness of parental childlessness to the implications in their own lives. Like adoptees before them, donor offspring have to decide if they will open themselves up to an honest exploration that may cause them deep sorrow and hurt their existing family relationships, while possibly bringing no tangible benefits, or if they will remain in a protective cocoon of silence or denial, to save themselves the trauma of dealing with the truth. Regardless of the dearth of studies which could effectively quantify serious residual negative issues in the lives of all parties concerned, the potential for such problems cannot be dismissed.

Openness

In recent years some "experts" and donor parent support groups around the world have been encouraging greater "family openness" and supporting legal changes to bring an end to anonymous gamete donation. The latter came into effect in the UK on 1 April 2005 after much lobbying and the success of the High Court case of Joanna

---

[7] At a convention in Sydney in November 2001 organised by the Donor Conception Support Group in Australia, only two of the 19 adult donor offspring present had parents who were still married.

Rose and E (a child) versus the Secretary of State for Health & the Human Fertilisation & Embryology Authority, where Mr. Justice Scott-Baker ruled that "an AID child is entitled to establish a picture of his identity as much as anyone else". That picture will, of course, remain fuzzy and distorted for the first 18 years. Unfortunately the new legislation, unlike that implemented for adoption, is not currently being applied retrospectively because the privacy of donors and their families is considered to take precedence over the identity needs of donor offspring. Effectively a further level of discrimination and injustice has been imposed on older offspring. No steps are being taken to gather old records from private practitioners or NHS repositories, which might be used to provide non-identifying information to adult offspring for whom even small fragments of information about their biological fathers would be most welcome. Both of these omissions urgently need to be addressed.

The UK Voluntary Exchange and Contact Register Following Donor Conception Pre 1991 (UKDonorLink) was launched in March 2004 and hopefully will be of benefit to a small number of the more recently born donor offspring, whose biological fathers, mothers or siblings are willing to come forward to offer information about themselves or even to establish contact. This service, currently running for a trial period, is small consolation for the egregious wrong which has befallen donor offspring, and one which would be more acceptable if accompanied by a full and unreserved apology from the government and medical profession for the reckless way in which reproductive services have been conducted: without due concern for the most vulnerable party. Potential adopters are required to jump through hoops to prove their appropriateness to parent a child who has inadvertently become a victim of kinship severance, yet private fertility clinics require little more than a credit card before "treatment" is approved. The long-term welfare of people conceived by donor gametes must always be shown paramount concern. If such a policy was to be properly implemented and full consideration given to the best interests of the non-consenting future person, it would be difficult to see how clinics or would-be parents could justify the deliberate separation of their intended child from any section of its biological family to appease their own involuntary childlessness.

In view of a lack of evidence to show that donor conception is of therapeutic value to the child deliberately created through it, along with a growing body of testimony to suggest that it may be both directly and indirectly responsible for negative consequences which impinge upon that created person's life, there is urgent need for a thorough review. The state-sanctioned and entirely intentional breaking of biological bonds through donor gamete technology can only be counted as an ethical choice if society genuinely believes, based on scientifically proven principles, that blood relationships have no special relevance.

In my opinion, true family and social openness cannot be achieved unless commissioning parents are forced to face up to their actions by formally declaring the use of donor gametes on their child's birth certificate. While it might seem that the openness policy now generally encouraged by service providers is being pursued for the benefit of the affected children, some might view the move as a cynical ploy aimed at protecting the fertility industry and its main beneficiaries in the new climate of Human Rights legislation, by which the public might have recognized the use of anonymous donor gametes as an indefensible moral wrong. Italy, with its more humane and Catholic approach to human reproduction, outlawed the use of all donor gametes in 2004 and banned the creation of excess embryos. Under their new regulations the right of adults to procreate and "found a family" as nature intended has not been denied, but their access to certain treatments which disrespect some of the most basic principles laid down in the United Nations Convention on the Rights of the Child has been withdrawn.

Exploitation

Much as I still have every sympathy for those who are not "blessed with children", there is simply no way to adequately balance the parenting aspirations of adults who require donor gametes against the long-term side-effects of family rupturing and identity deprivation for the resulting vulnerable and non-consenting party. The frustration of one generation does not justify the complications that donor conception bestows on the next. Even the gamete donors are being exploited by the system, which induces, under the guise of social benevolence, the extraction and reassignment of the basis of their biological children. While sperm donation is not exactly an onerous task, the altruistic donation of eggs requires an invasive and potentially life-threatening medical procedure. There are more losers than winners in the donor gamete triad.

I cannot support an industry that assigns parentage without regard for blood kinship. The routine manipulation of human gametes has allowed the very essence of life to be exploited, commercialized, demeaned and debased. The previously unseen human embryo is now a collectable, valuable resource. We all thought slavery had died out in the days of William Wilberforce, but in the twenty-first century we are allowing proto-people to be swapped, bartered, shipped across international boundaries, experimented upon, defrosted and sold like fashionable consumer commodities. I firmly believe that one day, but perhaps not in my life-time, society will look back, as I do now, at the current explosion in "reproductive choices" with disgust and dis-belief, and wonder how anyone could have deluded themselves that assisted reproductive technology was morally justified, within a supposedly civilised society.

REFERENCES

Snowden, R, Mitchell, G D and Snowden, E M (1983) *Artificial Repro-duction: A Social Investigation*, Allen and Unwin, London

Turner, A J and Coyle, A (2000) What does it mean to be a donor offspring? The identity experience of adults conceived by donor insemination and the implications for counselling and therapy. *Human Reproduction* **15,** pp. 2041–51

The DI journey: pain, loss and discovery

You shall know the truth, and the truth shall set you free.

Louise Jamieson

INTRODUCTION

I share in this article some of my experiences, perceptions and conclusions about being donor-conceived.

Much of the story is intensely personal. In some places I relate insights which, though highly subjective, have helped me make sense of my life. I have found the writing very difficult. It has taken time to try to put my deepest feelings into words. Constantly at the back of my mind is the knowledge that many are sceptical about the difficulties of growing up as a donor-conceived person, and resentful of reform which has threatened the supply of sperm. I have also wished so far as possible to remain loyal to my parents, whilst being honest about the difficulties I encountered – a significant tension.

I speak from the perspective of an older DI adult. It has taken me until middle age to find the emotional strength and independence to unravel the threads of my family background. There may be little in common with the experience of a younger DI-conceived person, particularly if they have always known about their origins. On the other hand, it may be that, as they get older, they will encounter some of the same thoughts and feelings in themselves.

MY STORY

The trapdoor opens

I was 32 when my mother told me I was donor-conceived. Sitting in a hotel room in Paris on a wet Wednesday, she had asked me what I intended to do with the rest of my life. I had just received a voluntary redundancy payout, and the world was my oyster. I had done all the exercises you're supposed to do when changing life direction – asking myself about my motivations, passions and interests – and had come to the realisation that my life to date had been driven by a desire to belong. That had fuelled both my job choices, and my behaviour in those jobs. I explained this to my mother, and started to cry. "I guess it must be because I'm an only child, though I know you and Dad couldn't have any more kids."

It was at that moment that Mum was compelled – or perhaps propelled is a better word, as the energy seemed to come from outside herself – to tell me. "There's something you need to know: Peter's not your father."

I was quite calm in my response. "Isn't he?" It wasn't anything like a blow to the heart; I didn't feel winded. It was more like a dark fog beginning to dispel. Or the ground gently giving way under my feet.

In two, maybe three seconds, I did a lot of emotional computing. Years before, in a moment of adolescent bullishness, I had asked my mother if she'd ever been unfaithful to my Dad. She hadn't (she had been so brutally honest about her past in other respects, that I had no reason to doubt her on this). So how had I been born?!

She explained that when they married she knew that my Dad would be unable to father children, owing to a botched operation some time before. It had not bothered her. Four years later, broodiness struck. With my Dad's blessing, Mum wrote to an agony aunt, who sent back the names of two London fertility clinics. In what she considers one of her best decisions ever (Mum was and remains very pleased with me as a finished product!) she opted for one of those clinics. I was conceived on the second attempt.

Since the age of twelve or thirteen, I had reacted violently to donor insemination whenever it was mentioned on the TV (it had always seemed to me an absurdity that people should simply *pretend* someone was somebody else). But it had never crossed my mind that I could be conceived that way. I did not think it had been around in the early sixties.

Hearing about DI, my response changed. Instead of a gentle landslide, I felt a trapdoor fall open at my feet. All my life, I had felt as if I was standing on a false floor and could not get to the real stuff

31

underneath. It was like floating a few feet above the ground with no place to stand. As the trapdoor released, the false floor fell away revealing a black vacuum underneath. At the same moment I had a mental image of a birdcage door opening onto blackness and freedom. I went into the bathroom to get something to mop up my tears. I had often stared at myself in the mirror, paralysed by the idea that this was "me" – whoever "me" was. Now as I caught sight of myself in the mirror I felt for the first time ever as if I was truly looking at ME and, even more surprisingly, liked the person I saw there.

Secrecy

At my Mum's instigation, my parents had for 32 years covered up the truth about my conception. Dad wanted to begin to tell me when I was five, but my mother's sense of shame – or at least embarrassment – prevailed. In some ways I can sympathise with her. They lived in a small town, with friends and relatives not distinguished by their open-mindedness. The choice of secrecy meant at least that I grew up without stigma, free from knowing looks or mutterings.

My mother's insistence on secrecy was also in line with the received wisdom of the "experts". The clinic had declared that I must never be told. I guess that, as with adoption, the child was considered a clean sheet. Absorb them into a loving family, hide from them unpleasant facts about their origin, and everything will be okay.

I never questioned that Peter was my father. I knew we were nothing alike, and can look back at the rather pathetic relief and gratitude I felt whenever I noticed some minor physical resemblance or shared trait. I had very little in common with the cousins on my father's side, but only ever put this down to differences in family circumstances. I took after my mother physically and emotionally and assumed as I grew older that her family genes were outstandingly dominant!

Premonitions

Underneath my conscious acceptance of the family story, I had many subconscious intimations of something different. I remember as a child going to church and thinking how strange it was that Peter was my father, but not the father of the other people there. I was in some way latching onto the arbitrariness of our relationship and trying to make sense of it. I always felt ill at ease with my surname and wished I could be called by my mother's maiden name. From puberty I had a recurring dream that I was pregnant, or had given birth to a child, without having had sex. The dream was filled with distress and shame as I cast around to find an answer to the riddle.

I never suspected a family secret. Yet I did live in fear of somehow being "found out". I was convinced that my mother knew something terrible about me which she could see, but which she did not tell me. I assumed it was some heinous character flaw. I remember saying to Dad when I was 15, "If we weren't related we probably wouldn't get on" – I am horrified now to think how cutting those words must have been.

Self-hatred

My Dad and I had a fairly good relationship when I was a young child. I remember feeling deeply aggrieved when he disciplined me, but other than that we got on pretty well. We spent a lot of time thrown together both for company and for household chores because of my mother's prolonged ill-health.

When I became a teenager the cracks began to show. I often felt he denigrated people or interests that I valued. Conversely, I felt that I should be more like him – practical, efficient and tough. I could not work out why I had not inherited any of his strengths or abilities. There seemed to be only one answer: I was a useless person. For years afterwards, no matter what was happening in my life externally, I maintained the image of myself as wrong, a failure. I still catch myself waiting to "grow up" into the sensible, organised person I feel I should be. Obviously, relationships with biological parents can and do produce similar problems. It seems likely, however, that the lack of a genetic link increases the likelihood of parent/child dissonance:

> If they have the luck of the draw, they [adopted children] will find themselves placed with parents of similar temperament, talents and physical characteristics – parents who are empathic to their needs.[1]

---

[1] Lifton, 1994, p. 60.

33

Not all adoptees have the luck of the draw. My father utterly did his best by me – always responsible, generous, as loving as he could be. But we had so little by way of shared personhood. I longed to be affirmed for the parts of me which were different from him. But I think it was difficult for my parents even to *see* great chunks of my personality, as they did not know what they were looking for. It is like the mother of an adopted child recalling:

> I watched him grow like a plant whose name I had forgotten ...
> I didn't know what he contained.[2]

I suspect I pushed myself into exaggerated identification with my mother, as the one parent in whom I could see myself reflected. Yet parts of me are derived from the black void of my unknown biological father.

Beneath the trapdoor

The eighteen months after learning of my conception were the darkest of my life. It was almost certain that I would never be able to trace my natural father, and that knowledge sat like a black hole inside me. Sometimes, the sense of not knowing who he was, and my own consequent lack of identity, would sweep over me physically. I would become light-headed and the whole world would seem unreal. I could think of no way out of the black hole and there was no one to help. I remember crying uncontrollably and frequently during that period, often feeling unable to share with friends or onlookers the reason for my behaviour. (I was, and remain, under the shadow of my mother's intense self-consciousness regarding my origins, and walk a tightrope between expressing my own emotions and respecting her fear of exposure.)

At other times, I would be hit by a sense of personal rejection. What was, from my natural father's perspective, a simple donation of sperm felt to me like deliberate abandonment.

It was a time of terrible aloneness. I knew nothing of DI support groups. I did not know a single other DI adult. I knew it would be pointless to contact the clinic to request information. I tried to lobby the Department of Health, but was, sadly, met first with inefficiency (as my

---

[2] Lifton, 1994, p. 45.

correspondence was lost), then with indifference. I knew that I lacked the financial and emotional resources to begin my own investigations, as some other DI adults have done. My one hope was that, in time, natural justice would compel the authorities to set up mechanisms to support the reuniting of blood relatives. In 2004, legal pressure did lead to the formation of the UKDonorLink Voluntary Contact Register.

In spite of these overwhelming feelings, at no point did I regret having been told the truth. For years I had battled with indistinct depression, chronic lack of confidence and a recurring sense that I did not "fit". Friends had urged me to receive counselling, but, tuning into some instinct, I had always replied that I would go when the time was right. I am grateful that I did not waste time, money and energy seeking answers when the problem had not yet been defined. Now, at last, I had a place of reality to work from, even if that place was the void under the trapdoor.

I consider myself deeply fortunate to have been told the truth about my conception. Withholding the truth from DI-conceived people is, I believe, cruel. If someone has a physical problem, it does not help to keep from them the name of their condition, or to assure them that there is nothing wrong. In fact, such a cover-up makes things worse, as the person now feels mad as well as sick! While it would be arrogant of me to suggest that every DI person is emotionally or psychologically affected exactly as I was, I believe it is equally naïve and belittling to suggest that people growing up in such complex family units will easily develop strong mental health. The least we can do to support them is to share with them the truth about who they are and who they are not.

Towards a solid base

Eight years on, I no longer feel I live in the black hole. My sense of identity and well-being no longer depend on discovering the identity of my natural father. But reaching this point has been a huge and diffi-cult journey. Without faith in a God who is Father, I think I would still be floundering. The support of groups such as the Donor Conception Support Group in Australia, DCAdultsUK and Bloodlines has been invaluable. A number of counsellors and pastors have listened to me, authenticated my feelings and experiences, and helped me acknowledge and process different facets of donor conception, as well as other family and individual issues. I have fleeting but ever more frequent glimpses of a new me, grounded in self-acceptance and able to relate to my parents as a more integrated adult.

The lie that I was Peter's child began even before I was conceived. I believe that this was like a straightjacket around my developing personality, in utero and beyond. It never felt safe to be me. I restricted myself in expressing emotion. The incredible effort it took, both before and after I knew about my origins, to relate to my father probably contributed to difficulties engaging in opposite sex relationships. I would automatically seal off the real me, searching for an acceptable persona, and striving to fulfil the other person's expectations. Conversely, whenever I met anyone with whom I felt genuinely, spontaneously comfortable, I would feel guilt and disloyalty, and sabotage the connection.

Harder to convey, and perhaps harder for others to believe, are the effects of DI itself *as a method of conception*. I gradually became aware of a habit of compulsive independence, dating back as far as I can remember. When I was a child, this manifested itself partly as a dismissive attitude towards my mother. In my adult years, apart from scuppering relationships, it bred a kind of masochistic overdrive in work, mirrored by difficulties in letting go and relaxing. Initially baffled by the compulsion, I eventually related it to the sense of aloneness I had felt from earliest childhood. Unable initially to find the root, I realised that it had set in even before I was born. My entry into the world was so anonymous. I am not merely referring to the protected anonymity of donors: I mean the physical absence of my natural father. How much in this I was picking up my mother's own feelings of confusion or ambivalence about my conception I shall never know. What I do know is that, since recognising the event of conception as a source of trauma, I have felt much more solid and secure in my own self, and in my relationships with others.

Have we seen it all before? Adoption

In one, major respect DI is utterly different from adoption. The DI-conceived have been raised by our birth mothers and we have not suffered the "primal wound"[3] of separation from her.

---

[3] Verrier, 1993.

DI offspring and adoptees do, nonetheless, share many things in common, and I generally think of myself as a "half-adoptee". Wanting to determine whether my own struggles were akin to those of full adoptees, I recently began to try to familiarise myself with some of the adoption literature, starting with the work of the American author, researcher and counsellor Betty Jean Lifton (who herself uses the term "half-adoptee" to describe those separated from their natural fathers).

I strongly identify with a distinction which Lifton draws between the "Artificial Self", created by the adoptee to maintain social family cohesion, and the "Forbidden Self", which derives from the unknown shadows of the child's biological parents. The "Forbidden Self" is often synonymous with the "real self", defined by the psychoanalyst Karen Horney as "the alive, unique, personal centre of ourselves that wants to grow".[4] Children can cut off from the real self when it is perceived to be incompatible with the needs of others. My own childhood and early adulthood were characterised by compliance and an almost infinite flexibility of character: I compulsively hid my own feelings and desires.

The American adoption system is still closed, so Lifton's reflections are particularly relevant to the experience of DI adoptees born pre-2005 under a regime of donor anonymity, and to a culture where DI children have been conceived, much as babies were adopted in the past, to address infertility problems. Both closed adoption and anonymous insemination rely on "the myth ... that love conquers all"[5]: that all that matters is that children are adopted by or born to parents who will give them everything they need materially and emotionally. Unfortunately, this is a mistaken belief.

> Implicit in the parents' loving message to the child is: "We will love you as our own unconditionally – under the condition that you pretend you really are our own".[6]

> When adoptive parents deny the reality of a difference between [a] biological child and the adopted child, they think they are

---

[4] Horney, 1950, quoted in Lifton, 1994.
[5] Lifton, p. 9.
[6] Ibid, p. 50.

assuring the adoptee of their love, but they are, in effect, denying the adoptee's reality.[7]

I myself have felt a spasm of pain every time my father has asserted that he "could not love me any more" if I were his natural daughter. I appreciate the generous intentions behind this statement, but feel utterly negated as the person who is, in truth, *not* his child. In claiming me for himself I feel he is depriving me of permission to access all the hidden, unknown parts of me which derive from my biological father.

Central to the well-being of a half- or full-adoptee is the acknowledgement of their unique story. The pain of the truth is infinitely preferable to the tensions and neuroses of living out a lie.

Plea

Many of us conceived from DI have experienced severe distress. I can, therefore, only begin to imagine what might be the experience of the offspring of different forms of surrogacy, as they grow into adulthood and maturity. I cannot bear to contemplate the issues of identity and self-hood to be faced in years to come by anyone finding themselves a product of cloning. As a DI adult, I want to sound a warning bell. The babies who "solve" today's infertility problems will have their own, long lives to lead. I foresee a correlation between the tangling of their family lines, and later confusion, pain or dysfunction, not necessarily during childhood, adolescence or even early adulthood, but almost certainly in later life. As part of the first "wave" of assisted conception, I feel I bear a responsibility to speak for those who are the products of newer techniques, and to urge greater circumspection on the part of the fertility industry and policymakers.

THE BIGGER PICTURE

Donor Insemination in the UK

The case of Rose v The Secretary of State for Health and the HFEA in 2002 established that the Human Rights Act was engaged in the

---

[7] Ibid, p. 55.

question of donor anonymity. This appears to have been a crucial trigger for the Department of Health's long-promised review of donor insemination. In 2004 the decision was taken that from April 2005, only donors willing to be named would be used. This represents an enormous leap forward for the rights of donor-conceived people.

There has been much subsequent media reporting of a decrease in donor numbers, and the Government is committed to improving and financing donor recruitment. The hard-won right to restrict DI to identifiable donors has already come under threat. Whilst I understand that infertility is an agonisingly painful issue, this does not give parents, clinicians or Government the right to deny children their identity.

Retrospectivity

The Department of Health Review ruled out any retrospective removal of donor anonymity for those of us conceived before 2005. This restriction of the Review's terms of reference was very disappointing. On the surface, the case is cut and dried: donations had been made on the understanding they were anonymous (it was, in fact impossible to donate *other* than anonymously[8]). That is fine, provided those giving the undertaking have the moral right to do so. There has, however, been no public exploration of whether it is appropriate to give protected anonymity to a consenting adult donor, at the expense of a future child who is not party to the decision, and who will, for his whole life, bear the consequences in terms of incomplete identity and possible psychological dislocation.

Parental discretion

Nothing in the amended legislation provides for donor-conceived children to be told about their origins. The social father continues to be named on birth certificates, which contain no indication of the child's DI status. Whether or not to "tell" is still left wholly to parents' discretion. The lifting of anonymity is null and void for the vast majority of those conceived through DI who are never told the truth.

---

[8] Rushbrooke, 2004, pp. 13–22.

As Rupert Rushbrooke has demonstrated, failure to acknowledge DI on birth certificates also blocks formal research on the long-term effects of DI, since the vast majority of donor-conceived people are never told the truth.[9] As a result, Lord Winston and others can claim that there is "no academic evidence" of the harmfulness of DI.[10] The fertility industry has itself ensured that such evidence cannot be collected.

For the lifting of anonymity truly to impact on those it is intended to help, birth certificates must be reformed, to provide for honesty and transparency *for all.*

Open DI

Personally, I feel in no doubt that the least harmful scenario for those conceived through DI – and ultimately, I believe, for their social parents as well – is one where the child is told the truth from an early age, and where identifying information is available about the donor (I know that under the new legislation this is possible only from the age of 18). Ideally, I would also wish to see the option of a face-to-face relationship with the donor from early on. The removal of donor anonymity in the UK has brought DI more into line with adoption.

A crucial difference from adoption

However, one massive difference between adoption and DI is that, with adoption, the children are born to mothers who, for whatever reason, cannot raise them. In Britain today, it is accepted within social work that children should be removed from the natural family only when absolutely necessary, and even then, the child's need for continued identification with the natural family is whenever possible respected. Adoption, though geared, in years gone by, towards the wishes of adopting parents, has always existed to "catch" babies and children who, through unfortunate circumstances, find themselves in need of a home.

---

[9] Ibid.
[10] See e.g. Winston, 1999; Winston, 2002.

Assisted reproduction operates on a completely different assumption: that children can be supplied to meet the demand of prospective parents, and that at best a compromise can be reached between their needs and those of the commissioning couple. Rather than protecting children who have become parent-less through unhappy circumstances, assisted reproduction actually creates father- or motherless children. Ultimately, to talk of "balancing" the needs of parent and child is an absurdity: the very most that can be done is to make a child whose existence depends on its being deprived of a relationship with a natural parent – and then to go part-way towards restoring that relationship.

(The "oddness" of DI goes further. I remember my shock when I first realised that the pieces of my natural family could *never* be pulled together. Previously, I had somehow felt that, were I to meet my donor, the jigsaw would be complete. But, of course, he may have his own family through a spouse or partner. He almost certainly has other children dispersed who knows where through sperm donation – my half-siblings. My family is irreversibly scattered.)

In comparing DI to adoption, therefore, we are comparing a deliberately-created situation with an "accidental" one. In both adoption and DI, we are looking at damage limitation, rather than an ideal scenario.

Imagining the experience of open DI

I wonder what it would be like had I been conceived in an open system, growing up with information about my natural father, and in due course knowing his name, perhaps even meeting him. I am sure it would have been infinitely preferable to my actual experience of secrecy, followed by the brick wall of protected anonymity.

I imagine living with my social father, knowing something about, and anticipating in due course a meeting with, my biological father. Perhaps it would have elements in common with the experience of children of divorced parents, who grow up with a stepfather or mother. Just as step-children's experiences can range from the bitterly unhappy to the comparatively happy and secure, it is no doubt difficult to generalise about the experience of open DI. For myself, I can imagine the possible guilt of divided loyalties (two fathers), or role model confusion (who am I/should I be like?). Though openness represents the best option for those conceived, I doubt it will erase all the tensions implicit in DI.

Grateful to be alive?

Obviously, I would not be alive were it not for DI. However, this simple statement conceals a more complicated reality.

Someone with a painful disease or wound may be grateful to be alive. On the other hand, they may feel overwhelmed and preoccupied with their pain. In moments when the pain of fractured identity, lost kinship or family strain becomes intense, the DI-conceived person may not be glad to be alive, and may even feel angry that they were ever born. It can be hard to come to terms with a deliberate action, endorsed by the State and executed by the medical establishment, which has cut one off from one's natural family, and resulted in one's natural father and mother never having even met. Feelings of anger and dislocation do not stem from ingratitude, but from pain.

SUMMARY

It is clear from the above that I find it difficult to perceive donor conception as a "treatment". For me, it has been a source of pain *requiring* treatment.

To minimise the pain, there are certain ground-rules which, I believe, MUST be adhered to.

1. Maintain the exclusive use of named donors (teamed with a programme of education to discourage the use of anonymous gametes from overseas etc).
2. Reform birth certification to give *all* donor-conceived children equal rights to knowledge about their identity.
3. Recognise and provide for the long-term emotional and psychological needs of those conceived by DI and their families. LISTEN to what DI adults are saying, so that DI is no longer perceived merely as a fertility treatment, but is understood to have significant social consequences.

And, for the pre-2005 generations of DI children and adults:

42

4. Reconsider the question of lifting anonymity retrospectively.
5. Meanwhile, commit to the long-term funding and publicising of UKDonorLink.

POSTSCRIPT

Shortly after completing this article, I received a letter from UK DonorLink, the donor conception voluntary contact register, notifying me that a DNA match had been established between myself and several half-siblings. It transpired that among those half-siblings was the son by marriage of my donor, meaning that at a stroke I had found not only living half-siblings, but also the identity of my now-dead biological father – an outcome which I had not even allowed myself to dream of at the time of registering with DonorLink.

This discovery marked the beginning of what has been the most extraordinary period of my life: extraordinary not only for the intensity of my reactions, but also for the rapidity with which my thoughts change from day to day as I continue to process the news. By the time I registered with DonorLink, I felt I had worked through most of my identity "issues" – I certainly did not register in the belief that finding relatives and/or information about my donor would make me complete (though that had indeed been my feeling some time before). My expectation in registering had rather been that, were I to discover other donor-conceived half-siblings, that would be a joyful bonus.

Instead, however, I have found the impact of learning my biological identity to be profound. I did not realise that I felt ashamed, yet having a solid, biological/genetic identity lifted from me feelings of shame. From childhood I would stare in the mirror, dazed by feelings of unreality, repeating to myself "this is me", yet having no idea what "me" was. The day I learned about my conception I looked in the mirror and felt for the first time that I "connected" with my own face. Now, the restoration has gone a stage further: I look in the mirror and think (though probably with little justification!) "what a fine looking woman!" I feel absurdly more confident, and friends and family have noticed a freer, happier me. My mother even remarked that I no longer seem hell-bent on punishing myself for breathing! (Thankfully, she and my social father have rejoiced with me at the discovery, though I believe it has also triggered some anxiety in my father.) Suddenly, there is space for all the un-labelled or unrecognised parts of my personality, and I feel free to expand into all that I innately am.

It is exciting, strange and overwhelming coming to terms with a vast extended "family". Our conception pre-dated any form of clinical regulation of DI, and our donor appears to have been extremely prolific. It is odd knowing that there are still other unknown half-siblings "out there", many of whom probably do not even know that they are donor-conceived. In some ways, I find it easier that my biological father is dead, as I do not have to face possible rejection, indifference or even dislike. Nonetheless, I ponder his motives, and wonder what he would make of me were we to meet. There is a lingering sense of abandonment and rejection, though knowing his name and some minimal information about him has certainly taken the edge off such feelings. I am grateful that I and my fellow half-siblings are adults, able to explore this unusual process of personal re-definition and corporate reunion largely free of concerns about our parents' insecurities, or their possible desire to control the process.

Two or three weeks after learning the identity of my natural father, a picture unfolded in my mind which seemed perfectly to represent the three phases of my life – before I knew about my conception, after I knew, and after I learned about my father's identity. To begin with, I saw a small cramped room. This was my life before I was told I was donor-conceived. Somehow, although it appeared in every respect identical to the others, I had a sense that one of the walls was just a thin partition with goodness knows what behind it (this reminded me of the feeling I had always had of standing on a false floor, to which I refer in the article). Being told I was donor-conceived was the equivalent of receiving confirmation that the wall was indeed just a flimsy partition. But, without access to information about my natural father, I could not break down the partition. I knew there was something beyond it which was intrinsically mine, but clinical secrecy and legislative inflexibility had sealed it off from me. Finally, when I found out my father's identity, a sledgehammer was taken to the partition. The false wall disappeared, and I found myself in a huge, airy room, which I knew belonged all to me. I had reclaimed my true self.

Plugging the identity gap has, for me, gone a long way to removing the worst consequences of being donor-conceived. Nonetheless, as already expressed, complications remain, and I retain misgivings concerning the tensions or conflicts of loyalty and identity which might be associated with growing up under an "open" DI arrangement. The joy I felt upon learning my identity reminds me of the intense relief which ensues when an illness or pain finally passes. The passing of pain is no argument for deliberately setting up pain in the first place. My experience and that of many others underlines that use of anonymous donors was indeed painful for those conceived. It is still largely unknown what difficulties may, in time, be associated with use of named donor sperm.

REFERENCES

Horney, Karen (1950) *Neurosis and Human Growth: The Struggle Toward Self-Realization,* Norton, New York, quoted in Lifton, Betty Jean (1994) *Journey of the Adopted Self,* Basic Books, New York

Lifton, Betty Jean (1994) *Journey of the Adopted Self,* Basic Books, New York

Rushbrooke, R (2004) Donor Insemination: the secret experiment. *Bulletin of Medical Ethics* **196**, pp. 13–22

Verrier, Nancy (1993) *The Primal Wound,* Lafayette CA

Winston, R. This Foolish Threat to the Gift of Life. *Daily Mail,* 26 July 1999

Winston, R. Review of "Making Babies: Is there a Right to Have Children?" *Sunday Times,* 4 August 2002

Afterword

Many people – clinicians, scientists, policymakers, members of parliament, philosophers, lawyers and the media, make judgements about families where gamete donation has been used and then build clinical practice, health care strategies and policies on these judgements. If, however, they have themselves not experienced this kind of family upbringing it is difficult for them to understand what it is really like to be a donor-conceived person, knowing only half of who one is and experiencing secrecy and evasions about one's origins, and ultimately finding that the society in which one lives and its lawmakers have not taken heed of the possible consequences nor sought advice from those who really know the dilemmas and disadvantages of being a donor-conceived person. The three chapters in this publication provide a chance to find out more.

What this Afterword aims to do is to offer answers to the following questions:

(i) How far are the life histories of the writers typical of donor conception outcome?

(ii) How far does what is known from research about the attitudes and relationships of the parents of donor-conceived children and about their parenting dovetail with the descriptions of family life presented from the offspring's perspective in this publication?

(iii) Are there hidden "costs", inherent potential risks, ethical and human rights issues being sidestepped or ignored in these medical procedures?

The histories are unique to each writer in the sense that they are individuals in their own right, but a comparison of these histories shows that there are certain themes that recur in all three.

THEMES THAT EMERGE IN THE DI ADULTS' HISTORIES

Undercurrents in the DI families

These are described in different ways in the histories. In Joanna's case, she had known in her childhood that she was conceived from DI but had been told to keep it a secret. She describes these undercurrents as issues that were "tiptoed around" and were "mostly beyond communication". For Christine, who was denied any information on her donor origins, there was a feeling that "something unseen and unspoken was pervading my life" – an "aura" of "something is going to happen" – and a "feeling of separateness I endured as a child". There also was a feeling that there was "something around me that was not quite right" and that "everything sad or bad that had happened in my life was my fault".

For Louise, also unaware of her donor origins, there were "many subconscious intimations of something different" from the family story.

Clearly, there are many non-donor conception families where there are undercurrents. For donor-conceived children, however, such undercurrents are linked with feeling different from the rest of the family, particularly the social father and his kinship group, and yet wanting to belong.

Relationships with the father

Louise and Joanna describe difficulties in relating to their social fathers. For Louise there was puzzlement that she felt so different in appearance and temperament from her father: somehow she felt this was her fault.

Joanna writes particularly about her realisation, with sadness, that she had no particular affinity with, or resemblance to, her father or to his kinship group who were the relatives who had surrounded her throughout her childhood. She reports that later she realised that her own particular characteristics came from her biological father and his kinship group, many of whom could well look like her but about whom she knew nothing.

For Christine, her relationship with her father was limited to the first few years of her life, since he died when she was six. She reports that she never felt that she fitted into the pattern of his life nor that of his family, who had lived in a rural area near the town where she was brought up.

When Christine learned about the law of inheritance of eye colour in biology at school, she realised that her father's eye colour had not appropriately matched hers. By this time she had begun to wonder about her paternity. This led on to her puzzlement at what was written on her birth certificate, which appeared to confirm that her father was her biological father.[1]

These same themes emerge frequently in the histories now being recounted by other DI adults. Their desire to feel that they belong in their families runs alongside the question: "but why do I feel so different?" The recognition of physical differences, as well as differences in temperament, from their social fathers is frequently mentioned.

Physical appearance of DI adults and how they relate this to others in their wider family

All three contributors recount how they became aware that there were differences in their own appearance in relation to others in the wider family of relatives. When looking in the mirror, for example, they report thinking "Who am I?" "Where did I get these particular characteristics from?" Louise reports in her postscript her reaction to this when she recently learned about her biological half-siblings.

Metaphors and analogies used

Clearly, these vary from history to history, yet there is a consistency about them. The analogy of feeling herself or her mind somehow enclosed in "a box" is used by Joanna.

Louise uses different analogies to describe her feelings of uncertainty: the false floor, the trap-door opening when she learned of her DI origins, and the "small cramped room" being replaced by a "huge, airy room" when she made contact with her biological half-siblings and so learned about her biological father. In her postscript she writes how this discovery has given her a sense of feeling free – free to be herself.

For others who have spoken or written about their DI experiences, they describe how they feel there is a line down the middle of them

---

[1] The question of birth certificates will be discussed later in these comments.

or that they feel divided down the middle: one half they know well and the other half not at all. They describe their need to find this other half to feel whole; they search the faces in the crowds on the street or in the supermarket in the hope of finding their donor. This is very distressing for them, particularly when it coincides with the normal developmental stage of adolescence when they are seeking to establish "who am I?" However, the search does not cease with adolescence. It continues into later life, as is clear in the three accounts in this publication. Two of the writers, Christine and Louise, report – one in a postscript, the other in her mini-biography – how they have begun to resolve this situation over the period of writing their stories. For Joanna, she reports how she has searched for family members but to date without any success.

I. How far are the life histories of the writers typical of donor conception outcome?

Confirmatory evidence that the three histories in this publication are typical of the outcome comes from a published analysis of eighty to ninety life experiences of DI adults/donor offspring.

Life experiences of DI adults/donor offspring

The following review is based on an extract from an already published paper.[2] By interviewing DI adults and by scanning the findings from studies available often as academic theses but occasionally published[3] and the literature about personal biographies in newsletters, the media and elsewhere,[4] it is possible to gain access to the experience of approximately eighty to ninety DI adults. That number is continuously rising as more and more are willing and able to write and talk about their experiences publicly. Through an international network of support groups, a forum has become available whereby they can

---

[2] McWhinnie, 2001. This paper was commissioned to open the debate on "Gamete Donation and Anonymity" in *Human Reproduction*, the journal of the European Society of Human Reproduction and Embryology.

[3] Turner and Coyle, 2000.

[4] This survey covers the UK, Australia, New Zealand and what was available to me from the USA.

talk with other adults created in a similar way. Years of isolation can end and they find that there are others with similar experiences: anguish, frustration and anger. What is also important about this form of contact is that they can discuss the issues without involving parents or wider family, many of whom might view their attitudes as disloyal. Donor offspring themselves also found that they could not talk about their feelings earlier because of their own feelings of disloyalty to their parents – for example, in revealing the parents' secret about their infertility.[5] In these histories there are reports of puzzlement, something in the family relationships that had puzzled them for years; some evasions or some unanswered questions; or that they felt that their father was very distant from them. "Perhaps my mother had an affair." For some the question posed was "is it somehow my fault that I feel so different from him?"

No matter how they had found out about their donor origins, the reported reaction was anger, resentment at the lies and deceit, or sadness and a loss of a sense of self and of their identity: "my story was destroyed, it was taken away. I felt I was in a vacuum. Who else knew?" "We trusted our parents to tell us the truth and they had been told to deceive us."

A few had the experience that when they learned about their donor origins this resulted in total parental rejection and, for example, the removal of their names from a parental will. For one woman, the father's rejection took the form of not acknowledging her should they happen to meet in the street in the town they lived in (her parents had separated). It was as if the parent could only manage the parenting role so long as the DI remained a secret and the infertility issue was thus not exposed.

All DI adults wished they had been told much earlier. They want to have information about their donor, what he looks like, what he is like as a person, his education and interests and especially details about his health and his family health record. Some want to meet him at least once. It is a source of great frustration and anger that this will never be possible. For some, the quest for information about their donor father preoccupies them: they wish it solved so that they can get on

---

[5] This is an issue also identified by offspring created in more recent years.

with their lives. A recurring comment about their anger and frustration is that no one thought them important enough to keep records about their donor father and that the system was set up intentionally to deceive them and to make it impossible for them ever to know. Even their birth certificates say they are the child of the father who brought them up and not their "real father" in the biological sense. So, how can they find who their biological father really is, and how many half-siblings are there out there that they don't know about, as well as uncles and aunts?[6]

If they have children, they too want details about the donor, his health, interests etc. As the adult daughter of a DI adult said, "after all he is my grandfather. What can I tell my own children about him?" Thus DI can be seen as having consequences into the next generation and the one after that. Many ask why has this been ignored for so long.

As individuals, donor offspring emerged in this analysis as competent, intelligent, articulate and thoughtful about others and about their own predicament, as do all three writers in this publication. The words they use can express sadness and wistfulness, frustration and resentment, anger and puzzlement at the indifference of others. Whatever their individual experiences and the words they use to describe them, they all make it clear that they consider themselves to have been done a serious injustice and wish the matter rectified. The following quotations illustrate this:

> I long to know who my biological father is and to meet and speak with him at least once. I search for my half siblings in other peoples faces. I want to know the missing part of my family's history, but more than anything I need to know the other half of my ethnic background. Now that some of us are adults it is time for our voices to matter. We have a right to know our identity and to grow up in truth. (Woman aged 42).[7]

---

[6] This is gradually changing for those born in the UK prior to the 1990 HFE Act. A voluntary contact register was set up in 2004: UK Donor Link Voluntary Information Exchange and Contact Register. This was set up as a result of the Rose and EM court case brought under Human Rights legislation.

[7] Speaking for Ourselves, 2000.

They created me in the same way as they breed pigs. All I know and am allowed to know about my father is that he masturbated his 'sample' for a sum. Yes you could say I'm angry. DI adults must be allowed to speak and must have rights and access to information on their genetic heritage. (Man aged 33).[8]

A series of videos are now available which illustrate the issues raised in the above analysis.[9]

II. How far does what is known about the attitudes and relationships of DI parents and about their parenting dovetail with the descriptions presented from the offspring's point of view in this publication?

Although DI (originally called AID, or Artificial Insemination by Donor) has been available as a medical provision for 50 to 60 years, no systematic follow-up studies were ever done, even though these were called for by two of the committees of enquiry[10] set up to consider the desirability of the use of Donor Insemination in humans. Its successful use in animal husbandry had already been established and had been quickly accepted. It was assumed that, transferred to humans, it would also be problem-free.[11] Those who had become parents by it were very satisfied and often returned for further children. The divorce rate was reported as lower than in the rest of the community, although how this was ascertained is not clear.

Parents were advised to keep the matter a secret and not to tell the children since it might be upsetting for them. It was argued that if

---

[8] Ibid.

[9] (a) Two videos give details of donor offspring's life experiences; (b) two record parental views and experiences of being open with their DI children – covering how they made the decision to tell their child, issues for infertile men, children's questions and conversations; (c) one is a documentary of a donor offspring's search for her donor father together with record searching, publicity and ultimately meeting possible donor fathers; and (d) the last is from an international conference in Toronto where donor offspring recounted their experiences. For details of origin and availability of these videos see notes at the end of the reference section.

[10] Feversham Report, 1960; Peel Report, 1973.

[11] McLaren, 1973.

they did not know, they would not ask about the donor. In any case, all donors were anonymous.[12] Registering the child's birth as if he or she were the genetic child of both parents presented a dilemma since it gave false information and was therefore breaking the law.[13]

Over the next decades, provision of DI expanded as part of fertility provisions in the UK and elsewhere in the world. It was only in the 1980s and 1990s that follow-up studies of DI began to appear. These studies fall into two groups:

(a) Those that address the psychomotor, behavioural and emotional adjustment and development of the children. The tests and questionnaires used to ascertain this are standardised measures based on norms for particular ages and stages of child development.

(b) Those that study interpersonal relationships and explore the social, psychological and emotional aspects of infertility, parenting and child-rearing. These use qualitative research methods, such as interviews and life histories. It can be argued that such an approach is particularly helpful when exploring new areas of complex human interactions such as creating children by DI and parenting the children created.

It is these latter studies which are especially relevant in answering the question raised in this section. However, as the first, "quantitative" group of studies are those most frequently presented at medical conferences, quoted in the medical press, and by the media, and used in the contemporary debate about ART, some detail on these studies will be given.

(a) Psychomotor, behavioural and emotional adjustment and development studies

The early studies in this group were follow-ups from particular clinics of young children on the basis of standardised tests already available.

---

[12] CIBA Foundation Symposium, 1973.

[13] This dilemma was resolved from the parents' point of view in 1987 when the Family Law Reform Act was passed; in it the registration of donor births showing the social father as the father became legal, provided the social father had given consent to the use of DI.

The findings showed the children developing within normal limits. Some studies, however, also included findings about parental attitudes. These showed that some social fathers were having difficulty in relating to their donor children, and also that there was a general tendency for parents to overprotect the children.[14] A number of comparative studies have also been done; for example, a sample of IVF, DI, adopted and naturally conceived children, at first when aged 4–8 and later when aged 12. A series of assessments were made – some by interview with the mothers, but others mainly by return of questionnaires. Also assessed was the level of attachment between the parents and the children. These studies showed again that the children were developing normally. It was also found that the IVF, DI and adopted children were more securely and appropriately attached to their parents than the naturally conceived children. On the basis of attachment theory it was claimed that these groups of children were better adjusted and "happier" than the naturally conceived children.

None of the DI parents had told the children about their origins, although a small proportion said they might do so in the future. Secrecy was viewed by the researchers as not necessarily deleterious to family functioning. The analogy with adoption was not viewed as relevant, on the grounds that adopted children have to come to terms with having been rejected by their birth mothers whereas ART children are wanted from the start. The basic finding was that "the presence or absence of a genetic link between parent and child was less important to the family relationships than the quality of the parenting".[15] Questions have, however, now been raised about these studies by Golombok et al, concerning e.g. the methodology and the lower participation rate[16] of DI families.[17] Other studies have failed to replicate the findings of superior parenting of ART children. It has also been questioned whether the ART and adoptive parents in these studies might have

---

[14] Kovacs, 1997; Ludwig, 2002.

[15] Golombok et al, 1995, 1996, 2002.

[16] A recent review of research studies of parental attitudes regarding secrecy and disclosure reported that only a minority of parents intended to tell the child of their DI origin: 14–19% (USA); 30% (Canada); 20% (Great Britain); 22% (New Zealand). Zoldbrod and Covington, 2000.

[17] Sutcliffe, 2002.

been more child-orientated from the start than those who had conceived naturally.

The findings from the social and interpersonal relationship studies certainly show a very different and much more complex picture, suggesting that reliance on overt behaviour in childhood and self report questionnaires about couples and their personal relationships do not represent the real complexity and dynamics of these families.

The reliance of Golombok's studies almost entirely on attachment theory can also be questioned as a predictor of long term outcome. It inevitably excludes other conceptualisations of adult–child interaction. Other researchers in the area of child development, in a review of other research studies and their own, commented: "theories ascribing overwhelming disproportionate and pre-deterministic importance to the early years are clearly erroneous".[18] Clarke and Clarke further comment that "there is no suggestion that what happens in the early years is unimportant. For most children, however, the effects of early experience represent no more than a first step on an on going path which may be straight or winding, incremental or detrimental depending on the two way relationship between individuals and their contexts".[19]

Also, a reliance exclusively on attachment and the emotional environment sidesteps the question of the relative weight to be given to nature and nurture. After a long period when environment was seen as all-important, studies relating to this issue have been extensively reported and reviewed.[20] They clearly have relevance for any discussion regarding the use of donated gametes. Plomin reports as follows: "research and theory in genetics (nature) and in environment (nurture) are beginning to converge. It is time to put the nature/nurture controversy behind us and to bring nature and nurture together in the study of development". Others writing in this area have commented that current estimates suggest that genetic influences account for anything between 30% and 70% of the variation between individuals.[21]

---

[18] Clarke and Clarke, 2000, p. 105.
[19] Ibid.
[20] Plomin, 1995; Rutter, 1999.
[21] Howe, 1995.

(b) Social and family relationship studies

Research by Snowden *et al* 1981, 1983; Baran and Pannor 1989; McWhinnie 1992, 1995, 2000, 2003 deals with the social, psychological and emotional aspects of parenting DI children. Snowden and Mitchell's study was based on the records of a DI clinic over a forty-year period, during which time 480 DI children were born. They also interviewed the parents who had children of pre-school age. Of particular interest here is that eight years later, when the children were aged 10–13 and a further follow-up was planned, 50% of the parents declined to participate, giving as their reasons fear of disclosure, or the fact that they never thought about DI and that to do so in a discussion would be "unsettling".[22] This level of psychological denial may be surprising to readers but it is in fact a finding of the two other studies in this group. Baran and Pannor[23] reported it as one of the main findings of their study. They concluded that the use of DI acted as a "cloak" for the man's infertility.

In my research studies (from infertility to IVF and DI parenting) I used in-depth interviews with both mothers and fathers where the children were at different developmental stages.[24] Parents reported that talking with me was the first time they had ever talked about DI, even with each other, since the day they had decided to use it. To the outside world, DI families appeared to be the same as any other family, both amongst friends and relatives and in the area in which they lived. The mothers had become pregnant and given birth, while the fathers were all present at the birth of the children. The parents said that there was therefore no need to tell anyone about the use of DI.

Parents reported developing strategies for dealing with any questions. For example, close relatives commenting about the baby, "I don't see anything of you in him" (i.e. the social father). The question of differences in physical appearance between the child and their father and between DI siblings frequently produced comments. The parents,

---

[22] Snowden *et al*, 1998.

[23] Op cit.

[24] A second, more structured interview was carried out to ensure comparability of the areas that had emerged as relevant. Full details about the methodology used and the findings can be found in McWhinnie, 2000(a).

nearly always the mother, either avoided giving a reply or found a distant relative that the child potentially resembled.

However, other incidents in daily living emerged which were much more difficult to deal with. The following are examples:

(a) In disputes over child care, in the hearing of the children, comments were made, for example, by the mother: "they are not yours, anyway"; by the father: "you can look after them, they are *yours* after all".

(b) A comment from an older step-sister who, on learning in a biology class about eye colour inheritance, asked why her new baby step-brother's eyes did not fit that inheritance law. The response from the mother was to burst into tears and hurriedly leave the room.

(c) Discussion amongst friends, critical about the use of donors to achieve a pregnancy, was dealt with by the father by determined silence. The mother's response was to suddenly leave claiming she was unwell.

(d) A recurring issue reported by the mothers was being asked at the GP surgery, when seeking medical advice about their child, "is there anything of this in the family?" The mother, of course, has no information available about the donor's family health history, so she replies, "not as far as I know". The danger of this misinformation was recognised if a serious health issue arose in the future.

The question of family health records is raised by Joanna in her contribution. She comments that not only is there no information but, of course, wrong information could be given since, in her experience, even although she knew she was conceived from DI, the details she gave were from her social father's family medical history.

Underlying these incidents is, of course, the man's infertility. In my study, I was able to learn from the fathers directly about their reactions on learning about their infertility. These ranged from disbelief, great sadness, a sense of inadequacy, to deep anger and, in one case, "blind rage". This was frequently combined with a desire that no-one should know. These reactions may seem surprising, as male infertility has become an acceptable topic for general conversation. The assumption has grown that male infertility can now be discussed openly. It is a very different matter, however, for the person actually experiencing it. They wish to avoid the humiliation of incurring frequently derisive comments from other men. This description of such reactions to male infertility is confirmed in other literature.[25]

The fathers' individual responses to their infertility clearly influenced how they responded as parents. For some, it resulted in an over-involvement with the child. They felt that they "couldn't do enough" for the child, and had a deep fear of being found out. This led, for some, to severe psychiatric problems, an insistence that on no account should the child be told, along with an acute conflict of conscience concerning religious teaching and a moral code of honesty. In one family, the preoccupation with the DI child was coupled with rejection of the already adopted child. The man's "subfertility" had been acknowledged in the case of the adopted child, but could be denied in the case of the DI child.

It is now frequently argued that if the children are told at an early age about their donor origins, none of the problems I have just described will arise. However, this is not borne out in a report of conversations with families where openness has been practised from the start: "Some parents acknowledged that the sadness of never having a biological child re-emerged intermittently, or was a background theme."[26] A DI father of two children (aged 17 and 14), in summing up his experience, said "there are mixed feelings, joy in the children you have and sadness for the children you did not have. Learning to live with the mixture is what it is all about".[27]

Clearly the data from the research studies already described shows that some DI parents, particularly fathers, manage this badly, while others deal with it by secrecy, evasion or denial. Children notice these reactions, and over time will work out their own interpretation of what is or could be the answer. Frequently this is that their mother may have had an affair.

From these findings it can be seen how the family relationships mirror and confirm the issues raised by the three main contributors' descriptions of their family and growing up experiences. They show

---

[25] Mason, 1993; Lee, 1996; Claire, 2000.
[26] Pettle and Burns, 2002.
[27] Ibid.

there is much more to DI parenting and outcome than can be shown by the studies described in the first, quantitative group. The social and relationship studies show that secrecy is a major issue and is deleterious to parent–child relationships. It protects the parents from having to confront what is really involved in becoming parents through DI. Simply advising parents to tell the children about their origins, although clearly essential from the child's and DI adult's point of view, will not in itself mean that parents will follow that advice.

Whether DI children are told about their origins at an early age or not is only part of the picture. They are also affected by their parents' attitude to their infertility, which remains unchanged and which in fact caused them to use DI in the first place. They also have to deal with their own personal search to fill the gaps in their genealogical history. They seek a resolution of this in order to achieve a feeling of "wholeness", with no "dividing line down the middle".

Now that further complexities are emerging with the successful contact with half- siblings comes the realisation that there are in reality three adult figures in these families: the biological mother, the social father and the biological/donor father. The importance of this, and the reality of the wider biological kinship group in the form of half-siblings is clear. In Joanna's history she reports searching for this kinship group, and Christine and Louise both report having found this group. How this will all play out in their future lives will become the next chapter in their life experiences. What the implications are for the parents is also relevant, as is how far medical practitioners in this area will be prepared to acknowledge the realities of these findings.

CONCLUSION

Are there hidden "costs", inherent potential risks, ethical and human rights issues being sidestepped or ignored in these medical procedures?

Children from DI appear to the outside world to be no different from other children born in the UK. It may be assumed that they enjoy similar rights, but the histories and the findings just described show this to be a false assumption. Genealogically disadvantaged from the start and, given the current rate of non-disclosure by DI parents, likely to be denied information about their DI origins, they will, if asked, quote a family health record containing false information.

This could contribute to a medical misdiagnosis. With advances in knowledge of genetics and its relevance for health and other issues, this is something that troubles many DI adults. Also, should they wish to explore their family history, as many people now do, or if they sense a secret, and wish for information to resolve this, they are likely to take as their starting point the official birth records. These records will not, of course, in their case provide an answer. The only way they can get any information to begin a search is through their social parents.

All of this is clearly discriminatory and at variance with what is legally available to others. But more fundamentally, it is clearly contrary to the contemporary emphasis on children's rights and insistence that their voices should be heard. These rights can be claimed under the United Nations Convention on the Rights of the Child (1989). The relevant sections are article 7, "as far as possible the right to know and be cared for by his or her own parents", and article 8, "the right to preserve his or her identity including nationality".

The other avenue through which DI offspring's rights have been successfully defended is under Human Rights legislation. Under article 8 of the European Convention on Human Rights it has been argued that donor offspring have a right to respect for private and family life. The judgement was that "respect for private and family life requires that everyone should be able to establish details of their identity as individual human beings. This includes their origins and the opportunity to understand them. It also embraces their physical, and social identity and psychological integrity... A human being is a human being whatever the circumstances of his conception and an AID child is entitled to establish a picture of his identity as much as anyone else. We live in a much more open society than even 20 years ago. Secrecy nowadays has to be justified where previously it did not..."[28]

It is more than time that the voices and experiences of DI offspring should be recognised and listened to. They are as much "stakeholders" in the contemporary debate as clinicians, scientists and would-be parents. In fact, it can be argued that their experiences and views

---

[28] Rose and Another v. Secretary of State for Health and Human Fertilisation and Embryology Authority, (2002) WHC 1593.

should be given paramount consideration, since they carry for a lifetime the consequences of ART intervention: intervention which they did not choose nor consent to. This publication offers an opportunity to understand donor conception from their perspective and will, I hope, be widely read.

References

Baran, A and Pannor, R (1989), *Lethal Secrets*, Warner Books, New York

CIBA Foundation Symposium 17 (1973) *Law and Ethics of AID and Embryo Transfer*. Elsevier, Excerpta Medica, North Holland

Claire, Anthony (2000), *On Men: Masculinity in Crisis*, Chatto and Windus, London

Clarke, AM and Clarke, ADB (2000), *Early Experience and the Life Path*, Jessica Kingsley, London and Philadelphia

Family Law Reform Act (1987) HMSO, London

Feversham Report (1960) Report of the Departmental Committee on Human Artificial Insemination, HMSO, London (Cmnd 1105)

Golombok, S, Cook, R, Bish, A *et al* (1995) Families created by the new reproductive technologies: Quality of parenting and social and emotional development of the children. *Child Development* **64**, pp 285–288

Golombok, S, Brewaeys, A, Cook, R *et al* (1996) The European study of assisted reproduction families: Family functioning and child development. *Human Reproduction* **11**, pp 101–108

Golombok, S, Brewaeys, A, Giavazzi, MT, Guerra, D *et al* (2002) The European study of assisted reproduction families: the transition to adolescence. *Human Reproduction* **17**, pp 830–840

Howe, D (1995), *Attachment Theory for Social Work Practice*, Macmillan, London

Human Fertilisation and Embryology Act (1990) HMSO, London

Kovacs, G (1997) The Use of Donor Insemination, in Kovacs, G (ed) *The Subfertility Handbook: A Clinicians' Guide*, Cambridge University Press, Cambridge, pp 139–150

Lee S (1996), *Counselling in Male Infertility*, Blackwell Science Ltd, Oxford

Ludwig, M (2002), *Pregnancy and Birth After Assisted Reproductive Technologies*, Springer-Verlag, Berlin Heidelberg

McLaren, A (1973) Biological Aspects of AID and Embryo Transfer, in CIBA Foundation Symposium 17 (1973) *Law and Ethics of AID and Embryo Transfer*, Elsevier, Excerpta Medica, North Holland, pp 3–9

McWhinnie, A (1995) A Study of Parenting of IVF and DI Children: The Social, Medical and Legal Dilemmas, *Medicine and Law*, World Association of Medical Law **14**, pp 501–508 (Award-winning paper presented at 10th World Congress on Medical Law, 1994)

McWhinnie, A (1996) The Ethical and Legal Dilemmas in the use of Donor Gametes, included in Communications of the Participants at the 3rd Symposium on Bioethics of the Council of Europe, Strasbourg, December 1996

McWhinnie, A (1998) Ethical Dilemmas in the use of Donor Gametes. *Medicine and Law* **17**, pp 311–317

McWhinnie, A (2000a) Families from Assisted Conception: Ethical and Psychological Issues. *Human Fertility* **13**, pp 13–19

McWhinnie, A (2000b) Children from Assisted Reproductive Technology. The psychological issues and ethical dilemmas. *Early Child Development and Care* **163,** pp 13–23

McWhinnie, A (2001) Should offspring from donated gametes continue to be denied knowledge of their origins and antecedents? *Human Reproduction* **16,** pp 807–17

McWhinnie, A (2003) Disclosure and Development: Taking the baby home was just the beginning, in Singer, D and Hunter, M (eds) *Assisted Human Reproduction, Psychological and Ethical Dilemmas*, Whurr Publishers Ltd, London

Mason, M C (1993), *Male Infertility: Men Talking*, Routledge, London

Peel Report (1973), Report of the Panel on Human Artificial Insemination. *British Medical Journal Supplement*, April 2, pp 3–5

Pettle, S and Burns, J (2002), *Choosing to be open about donor conception: the experiences of parents*, Donor Conception Network, UK, p 13

Plomin, R (1995) Genetics and Children's Experiences in the Family. *Journal of Child Psychology and Psychiatry*, Annual Research Review **36/1**, pp 33–68

Rose and Another v. Secretary of State for Health and Human Fertilisation and Embryology Authority (2002) WHC 1593

Rutter, M *et al* (1999) Genetics and Psychiatry: I Advances in Quantitative and Molecular Genetics and II Empirical Research Findings. *Journal of Child Psychology and Psychiatry*, Annual Research Review **40/1**, pp 3–56

Snowden, R and Mitchell, GD (1981), *The Artificial Family: a consideration of artificial insemination by donor*, Allen and Unwin, London

Snowden, R, Mitchell, GD and Snowden, EM (1983), *Artificial Reproduction: A Social Investigation*, Allen and Unwin, London

Snowden, R, and Snowden, E (1998) Families created through donor insemination, in Daniels, K and Haimes, E (eds) *Donor Insemination: International Social Science Perspectives*, Cambridge University Press, Cambridge pp 33–52

Speaking for Ourselves – Quotes from Men and Women Created by DI/ Remote Father Conception. Collection made available to participants at Conference 'What about me? The Child of ART', March, 2000, held in London by CORE (Comment on Reproductive Ethics)

Sutcliffe, A G (2002), *IVF Children, The First Generation*, Parthenon Publishing, London

The United Nations Convention on the Rights of the Child (1989) Articles 7 and 8

Turner, AJ and Coyle, A (2000) What does it mean to be a donor offspring? The identity experience of adults conceived by donor insemination and the implications for counselling and therapy. *Human Reproduction* **15**, pp 2041–51

Zolbrod, AP and Covington, SN (2000) Recipient Counselling for Donor Insemination, in Burns, LH and Covington, SN (eds) Infertility Counseling: A Comprehensive Handbook for Clinicians, Parthenon Publishing Group, New York and London, pp 325–354

DETAILS OF VIDEOS AND AVAILABILITY

Videos (a) and (b) are from a series entitled *Families from Assisted Conception: How have they fared? Six families tell their story in conversations with Dr Alexina McWhinnie* (2001). Available from Dr Alexina McWhinnie c/o Chameleon Publications, Rolleston, 16 Cupar Road, Newport on Tay, Fife, DD6 8DF, UK; email: amcwhinnie@fastmail.fm

(c) *Are you my Father?* Frame Up Films (2001), Herne Bay, Auckland, New Zealand

(d) *The Offspring Speak*, Video of Conference in Toronto (2000). Available from Infertility Network, 160 Pickering Street, Toronto, ON, Canada, M4E 3J7

About the Contributors

Dr Alexina McWhinnie was, until her recent retirement, Senior Research Fellow at the University of Dundee in the Departments of Social Work and of Law. She is a social researcher with extensive experience in the area of assisted conception, including experience as an infertility counsellor on an assisted conception unit. She is the author of numerous papers on social and psychological issues in IVF and DI families. She has also researched and worked in the areas of adoption, foster care, access to origins of children of incest, and other areas connected to parenting and family relationships.

Joanna Rose is an adult donor offspring who took the issue of donor offspring's rights to the High Court in the UK, which ruled in her favour that "an AID child is entitled to establish a picture of his [her] identity as much as anyone else". She holds a social science degree, and has had placements at post-adoption services in Queensland, including an indigenous service to support and reunite members of the "stolen generations". Joanna is currently completing a PhD on the ethics, philosophy and sociology of DI. She enjoys canoeing, pottery, singing, playing the guitar and writing songs.

Christine Whipp lives in Devon with Michael, her husband of over thirty years, and their three second-hand cats. Her two adult daughters have produced (to date) five grandsons, so the anonymous sample of sperm from which she was conceived in 1954 is now responsible for the lives of eight people. Having discovered the identities of several men who may have provided sperm for the conception of babies at the clinic attended by her mother, she was able to persuade the surviving sons of one such man to undertake a DNA test to establish if she might be their half-sister. Thanks to the generosity of the two brothers, who agreed to be tested despite knowing that their father had always intended to remain anonymous, the search for her full identity has been accomplished. She now continues to be involved in the donor conception debate, and to encourage other donor offspring to seek information on their identities and biological heritage.

Louise Jamieson has worked as a civil servant, charity administrator and infant teacher, as well as spending two years in Australia studying drama and theology. Currently living in Oxford, she is enjoying forging links with new-found family members and finding out about her paternal family history. In light of her own experiences, she is very interested in the application of faith to issues of identity, and hopes to undertake further training in this area.